MW01199769

THE
BOOK
OF
signs

THE
BOOK
OF
signs

150 Symbols and Their Spiritual
Messages from the Other Side

MYSTIC MICHAELA

Author of *The Angel Numbers Book*

ADAMS MEDIA

NEW YORK AMSTERDAM/ANTWERP LONDON TORONTO SYDNEY/MELBOURNE NEW DELHI

Adams Media
An Imprint of Simon & Schuster, LLC
100 Technology Center Drive
Stoughton, MA 02072

First Adams Media hardcover edition
June 2025

For information about special discounts for bulk purchases, please contact Simon & Schuster Special Sales at 1-866-506-1949 or business@simonandschuster.com.

The Simon & Schuster Speakers Bureau can bring authors to your live event. For more information or to book an event, contact the Simon & Schuster Speakers Bureau at 1-866-248-3049 or visit our website at www.simonspeakers.com.

Interior design by Michelle Kelly

Manufactured in the United States of America

1 2025

Library of Congress Cataloging-in-Publication Data
Names: Mystic Michaela, author.
Title: The book of signs / Mystic Michaela, Author of The Angel Numbers Book.
Description: First Adams Media hardcover edition. | Stoughton, Massachusetts: Adams Media, 2025. | Includes index.
Identifiers: LCCN 2025000982 | ISBN 9781507223970 (hc) | ISBN 9781507223987 (ebook)
Subjects: LCSH: Signs and symbols. | Spiritual life.
Classification: LCC BL603 .M975 2025 | DDC 133.9/3--dc23/eng/20250127
LC record available at https://lccn.loc.gov/2025000982

ISBN 978-1-5072-2397-0
ISBN 978-1-5072-2398-7 (ebook)

DEDICATION

To Breanna and Abigail

Author's Note

Lying out in the sun one summer day, I felt compelled to look up into a nearby tree. There, staring at me with a fierce look in his eyes, was a hawk. We locked eyes for just a moment, but it felt inexplicably longer: a layered amount of time. He swooped down close to my head, and I felt the air from his flight rush by. I was left with a sense of profound emotion; there was significance in our exchange that words fall short to explain. This experience left me with a need to amplify my own relationship with the spiritual sources around us, which deliver messages. Writing this book is a way in which I have been able to do just that. I am grateful that I did not brush off that moment as just happenstance, and that I instead transmuted the emotion I felt that day into this guide of signs. Hopefully, in this book you will find inspiration to do the same—to receive the beautiful messages that are here to assist you, and to utilize them for transformation in your own lives.

CONTENTS

Part 1

An Introduction to Signs ... 17

Part 2

The Dictionary of Signs ... 37

Part 3

Signs Log ... 213

INTRODUCTION

Does it seem like dragonflies always appear when you think of a certain loved one who's passed on? Have you been noticing more images of cherry blossoms lately? Is a body of water often featured in your dreams? Signs are everywhere, from the tulips that seem to pop up wherever you go, to that recurring dream about a tiger, to the mysterious key you found when cleaning out the attic. These occurrences, however frequent or subtle, are messages sent to you from the other side.

There are many reasons why you may be receiving messages from a departed soul. Whether it is a loving relationship, a mutual passion in life, or something else you have in common, there is a bond to tap into further. And fortunately, connecting with the energy of those who have crossed over is an ability you have always had! It is a natural gift given to every being from the time they are born. However, many times these opportunities for connection and attempts by loved ones and other energies to communicate can go unnoticed, simply because you don't know what is being said.

The Book of Signs will help you decipher these messages. You will discover the tools you need in order to receive signs and understand the meaning behind them. In Part 1, you will learn more about what signs are, who may be sending them, and how they can appear in your life. You'll also explore the different types of signs: ephemeral and physical. In Part 2, you'll find a dictionary of 150 signs commonly used by those who have crossed over. Here you will also investigate ways to communicate back, as well as learn what you can do to make the most of the signs you receive. And in Part 3, you will start your own Signs Log, where you can record and reflect on the signs that show up in your life, connecting both with them and their messengers in ways that are personal to you and your experiences.

You are able to communicate with the other side; the next step is unlocking this talent. As you journey through the pages of this book, you will hone the language of signs for yourself!

HOW TO USE THIS BOOK

This book is divided into three parts, which encompass the experience of receiving, recognizing, and deciphering signs. The key factor in each step of the way will be your emotions, as well as any personal relationship you may share with the departed spirit who is sending you that sign. Your unique experiences, feelings, etc., are the foundation upon which these otherworldly lines of communication can build. With the guidance in this book, you'll be able to translate the mysteries of signs into a fluent language for navigating life and the amazing world around you!

In Part 1, you will learn more about what signs are, including different types of signs and how you may receive them. While many of the specific signs explored in this book fall in the "tangible" category (for example, an animal or a clock), non-corporeal signs, or signs that appear with no physical form (for example, an emotion that seems to come out of nowhere or a social interaction that makes a lasting impression), are also examined as wonderful aids in unlocking connections with those who have crossed over.

In the second part of this book, you'll find 150 signs and symbols commonly used by spirits on the other side to reach out. Although they will have varied meanings that differ between cultures, contexts, and any personal relationship you may have with the departed, this guide serves as a basis for connecting deeply with the other side. Use this part as a dictionary of sorts to quickly decipher the ways in which you're being signaled from those who have passed on.

Finally, in Part 3, through guided reflection you'll make sense of your own habits surrounding receiving signs. Here you'll find a log for tracking the signs you receive—along with your own emotions, connections, and intuitive feedback regarding them—so you can better understand what is being said and by who.

This book is a tool for you to use to amplify your own existing ability to perceive and receive energy from beyond the physical realm. You are about to begin a quest, exploring your natural world, inner intuition, and daily life for the treasures of messages hidden in plain sight. Once you see the ways in which spirits speak to you, the world will never look the same again! Let's begin.

PART 1

An Introduction to Signs

Your journey into the language of signs begins with understanding a few basics. In this part, you will learn what signs are, who exactly is sending them, and how you can receive them. When exploring these topics, you'll not only be better equipped to notice exactly how you are being contacted but also feel more confident in where the signs you encounter are being sent from.

Your own intuition and instincts will be the pillars of this part. The emotion behind the symbols, personal experiences, and attention to the senses are going to be your best tools. The more you lean into the powerful bonds all beings share, or the unique personal connection between you and the departed, the more you'll be able to have faith in the signs you see. And while most of the signs detailed in Part 2 are physical, becoming familiar with the uniquely non-corporeal (or abstract) signs also described will heighten your awareness of those on the other side, as well as the special messages they are sending you. This is a natural ability and a language your soul is already familiar with. In Part 1, you will simply awaken it!

What Are Signs?

When a person passes into the next world, the way they communicate changes. Without a physical body, they now rely on a different means of making their presence known in the physical world. One primary way they do this is through a sign, or any sort of object, emotion, or occurrence that holds a deeper meaning. A sign can be in the form of a symbol, natural phenomenon, or seemingly coincidental event. A dove landing on your windowsill, a rainbow appearing at an opportune moment, and an important event landing on a personally significant date are all examples of signs!

The emotional, sensory, and elemental worlds are the keyboards with which those on the other side type in order to share their stories, warnings, affirmations, and more with the living world. Without the barrier of words alone, so much more can be said through the use of signs.

Different Types of Signs

The other side sends two main types of signs: physical and ephemeral. Physical signs are the more obvious signs that can be seen and/or touched. They show up as objects, events, or living creatures. Seeing heart shapes throughout your day, finding your attention drawn to an advertisement that "coincidentally" has your late father's birth date on it, and a dragonfly landing on your hand at sunset are all examples of physical signs. The deeper feelings associated with these signs create the connection between you and whoever is communicating with you. Feeling the need to purchase and restore a particular antique chair and being compelled to pick up a coin that has appeared in your path are examples of physical signs whose meanings are reinforced through emotion.

Ephemeral signs are less tangible; they are sensed *only* through emotion and other non-physical things like sound and smell. They are experiences that can feel dreamlike or easily passed off as a coincidence or mistake if you aren't paying close attention. For example, randomly hearing the voice of your deceased aunt in your head and "accidentally" calling a friend by their late mother's name might seem like small coincidences, but are actually powerful signs! Ephemeral signs can be a lot harder to explain to another person without the tangible proof that physical signs provide, but the feelings that come with these signs can be intense—a portal straight to the departed soul who is reaching out. Your anxiety, mood swings, and overall feelings are of the utmost importance in recognizing and understanding ephemeral signs.

Who Is Sending Me Signs and Why?

Those familiar to you, like a deceased grandparent or sibling, often send you signs. Why? Most likely, it's simply to remind you of their presence, send you their love, offer a helpful suggestion, issue a warning, and/or maintain their bond with the physical world.

However, it's not just the people you had a personal relationship with who do so. If you happen to share a house, a job, or even a friend with someone who has crossed over, you are more than likely already receiving signs from them. In these cases, those on the other side are communicating in order to give you direction, information, and support. The shared bonds linking every person on Earth are the very threads upon which the departed pull. When you share a headspace, or a mission and passion, you're on the same vibration of those in the afterlife!

Why Are Signs Important?

Beyond the specific reasons that different signs are sent (to give you information, help you in your life goals, reassure or advise you to make a change, etc.), signs maintain an important connection. Attention is a powerful frequency—a high-vibrational force—and giving attention to anyone, whether they are living or have crossed over, means sharing energy. In particular, the amount of energy it takes for someone who has passed on to send this type of gesture is immense. Their emotions are transversing whole planes of existence to connect with you in your own reality!

You have an essential part to play in this symbolic exchange. Allowing yourself to believe in signs, understanding more about what they are, who sent them, and what they mean, is how you reciprocate this devoted effort. When you receive their messages with an open mind, you're giving the departed more momentum and space to connect. Just like a conversation flows better when two people are giving it equal amounts of energy, this conversation of signs across planes works much the same.

Signs also offer new inspirations and insights. After all, those who have crossed over have a unique perspective, and they want to share it with you! By listening to them, you are allowing yourself more opportunities to grow, learn, and enjoy the amazing possibilities this world, and the worlds beyond, can provide.

How Can I Receive Signs?

It is often said that "seeing is believing"; however, in the world of signs, that couldn't be further from the truth. In this journey of discovering and reading signs, you'll find that there are many ways to receive messages—not just through a visual symbol.

Cases of Mistaken Identity

Have you ever been out in public and been completely sure you saw someone you knew who has passed on? A complete stranger walking by you looking exactly like someone you have lost—perhaps even walking similarly, wearing their style of dress, or showing familiar mannerisms of the departed, only for the resemblance to seemingly vanish when you look again—is a strong spiritual signal.

Souls on the other side will often use something called "third eye interference" to get your attention, say hello, and simply send a little bit of love your way. Your third eye, or the space between your eyebrows, is a spiritual location: It is the eye of your soul. And it's through this eye that the departed can show you the veil between worlds. This means of sending signs can also be used with pictures, or in entertainment like movies. Looking at a random photo and seeing someone who has crossed over, only to look closer and be "mistaken" is another example of receiving a sign. Also, seeing an actor who you feel resembles the departed, even when other people completely disagree, is a more humorous way someone who has crossed over will play with sending you signs. When you are seeing someone who reminds you of a person you thought you would never see again, it's a way they are getting your attention.

Misspeaking or Mishearing

Have you ever wanted to call someone you know really well by a different name? Continuously calling your coworker, Jennifer, "Theresa," or referring to your neighbor's husband, Michael, as "Jeremy" isn't always a random slip of the mind. It can be frustrating to misspeak a name, especially when there is no logical reason to. In some cases, however, this seemingly human error is actually a way that someone on the other side is trying to communicate. If you are the one misspeaking, you might be a "conduit" (or spiritual vessel) for a message being sent to that other person. If you find yourself on the receiving end of somebody's misspeaking, it's possible *they* are the conduit for someone *you* share an otherworldly connection with. This is most apparent when you have an urge to call someone by a name that isn't theirs but feels appropriate for them. In this case, you may want to ask the person if the name you always have on the tip of your tongue means something to them.

Mishearing others is another means of "spirit interference." Thinking someone just said your departed best friend's name when they in fact did not, or hearing your childhood dog's name being called out only to hear it again differently can be significant. Hearing a name, fact, or phrase completely differently but with meaning to you is often an indication from the other side. The key here is your emotional response to what you think you heard. If you feel jarred or emotional all of a sudden, chances are someone who has passed on is making themselves known.

As with all signs, how often misspeaking or mishearing happens is something to consider when you're deciding whether something is a sign or a simple mistake. If you find it happening frequently, it may be more than just your distracted mind!

Emotions

While completely engrossed in your daily routine, do you ever suddenly feel a flood of emotions that doesn't have any obvious connection to what is happening? When someone passes, your emotions become the instrument they play to make you hear them from the other side. Feeling sudden and unaccounted joy, sadness, pride, love, elation, or even anxiety can signal their presence in your spiritual space. Looking out the window on a sunny morning and suddenly feeling the rush of their loss hit you as if it's new again, or laughing uncontrollably as you randomly recall a funny joke they once told you, is an example of their energy communicating with your own.

This can also happen even if the person wasn't familiar to you in life. You may find a room in your house feels "homier" than the rest regardless of how you decorate, or walk into an office space and suddenly be hit with a strong motivation to get to work—motivation that doesn't feel like your own. The key to differentiating spiritual interference versus your feelings acting of their own accord is thinking about what came before the shift in emotion. When it's a soul giving you an emotional sign, these flashes of feelings will be random, without connection to anything you were just doing, and seemingly out of nowhere.

You don't need to wait for spirits to communicate with you either; using your emotion, you can send signs of your own! For example, when you experience a feeling of love, loss, sadness, joy, or remembrance, it is a calling card to someone who's passed to join you in this very moment. Sharing mindsets can also set off this emotional connection to the other side. Feeling deeply motivated to fight an injustice after hearing a story of someone who perished because of it, and feeling the need to preserve the garden of the deceased former occupant of your house are ways emotion can connect you and allow you to communicate with the departed.

New Interests

Are you feeling a sudden interest in gardening, or an urge to read a genre of books your departed mother loved? People on the other side often make connections via new interests. The sudden desire to retile the bathroom floor like grandpa could, knit a sweater like Aunt Katie, or take on a community project you had no prior interest in is a way in which the departed communicate. Those who have crossed over can connect with the physical world more easily when you are doing something they themselves loved. You may feel closer to your departed mother when you become a parent yourself, or feel a desire to know more about the deceased entrepreneur who used to own the building your business is now located in. The wave of fresh energy toward an interest you didn't really know you cared about is often a nudge from their soul to yours!

"Ancestral pulls" are a unique feature of this form of receiving signs. You may find yourself suddenly very interested in creating a family tree, carrying on the stories of past generations, and updating records for future family members to have access to. In this way, you become a conduit for your ancestors, from those you knew in life to those who passed long before you were born. Oftentimes when you are reacting to ancestral pulls from the other side, you will want to not only research but actually go to the places your deceased family members lived in. Traveling to the homelands of ancestors is an impactful way those on the other side communicate with you and deliver insight, inspiration, and perspective unique to their own experiences, allowing their souls to live on in future generations.

Lost and Found Objects

Do you find yourself constantly misplacing objects you could have sworn you just saw? The frustration of losing an item you just had in front of you isn't unfamiliar to most people. However, understanding what it means when this happens often, and with objects of significance, can shift your entire perspective on why this is happening and who is causing it.

People who've crossed over can "borrow" objects. Slipping them in between the veil of this world and the next is one way of getting you to pay attention. And as annoying as it can be, it works. Understanding the reason for why an object is being borrowed by the other side can assist you in not just connecting with those who have passed, but also getting your item back quicker!

When missing an item of significance, such as your great grandmother's earrings or the ancestral family pocket watch, it's easy to think that perhaps you've just misplaced it. But when you know where you kept it and it has seemingly vanished, it's more than just your own mind playing tricks on you. It's a call from your loved ones on the other side. Often, they simply want you to slow down and remember them. Remembrance is what fuels the connection between this world and the next, and sitting in the moment and acknowledging the presence of the one you know is calling out to you can result in a return of the object—often in the exact same place you had previously not seen it.

Losing objects of importance, but not so much ancestral significance, can also be a sign from someone on the other side. This can be especially common in cases where you are "sharing" a home with a previous occupant who has since passed, or in a place of work where there is an active spiritual presence.

Frequently "losing" your car keys, important paperwork, or other necessary items and "finding" them in the same spot a few minutes later can be the departed playing a little trick on you. Take the moment of pause that the person who has crossed over may be asking for and give them a signal of connection that you both could use. Oftentimes, a little acknowledgment goes a long way in making sure these sorts of playful exchanges become less frequent.

Social Connections

Finding yourself wanting to send holiday cards to distant relatives you're not very familiar with? Or feeling the need to share gratitude with a group of people you barely know? Those who have passed on are often looking for others who are still alive to continue the things that were important to them. A sudden need to keep up with distant family members or interact with people who had special relationships with the departed is an example of someone sending you a sign from the other side. They are continuing to work on relationships they valued in life by disguising it as your own desire to make the same connections that they once prioritized.

This can be a rewarding connection between you and the departed, as you can feel their own excitement and happiness build in you as you forge social connections that were once their domain. The friendships and familial reach-outs can also be a rekindling of your own social calendar, especially if it's been lacking since the loss of that person.

Volunteering at the retirement home where your loved one spent their last years, picking up the project at work that a past coworker was invested in, and simply sending a holiday card to a family member your departed friend loved are all ways that the social connections of the person who passed are now being channeled through you.

Human Messengers

Have you ever had a child come up to you and say a special phrase that only someone on the other side would know? Ever had an illogical need to walk up to a complete stranger and give them an offer of support? Hearing a familiar saying or comforting word from a stranger isn't always just a happy coincidence. Many times, it's a departed soul channeling through another person in order to send a strong message of presence and reassurance. Just as with misspeaking a name or having a sudden urge to research your family history, those on the other side can use the living as conduits of their love. Sometimes this can happen with the other person's awareness, but oftentimes if you ask a person why they said what they did, they will have no clue that they said something unnerving—they just felt compelled to do so.

Actions are also ways in which a soul can use people as conduits of their own intentions. Meeting the right person at the right time to assist you in an important life endeavor can mean you're unknowingly working with someone on the other side. The teacher who sits with you a little longer to prepare for a test, a helpful and kind assistant at the bank, and a neighbor who regularly checks in on you are all examples of how the departed use human messengers to make their presence known. It's also not uncommon to receive special gifts from people that seem to have come directly from someone who has crossed over. Getting a baby gift from your coworker that looks a lot like something your late grandmother would have picked out and receiving important history about your house as you are remodeling it are signs that the person on the other side is actively still seeking contact.

Print, Art, and Other Non-Literal Mediums

Sometimes a sign will show up in an abstract (albeit very obvious) way. People on the other side have the ability to send you their messages by way of print, art, and patterns that grab your attention and curiosity. For example, a person who crossed over may have loved roses and you associate a special connection with them and this flower. Expect the unexpected when sensing their communication. Seeing roses not just in gardens, but in greeting cards received, in the form of jewelry, in a pattern on a shirt, or in an image on a billboard is a way the departed can get creative in their delivery.

Paying attention is your best means of spotting these signals. Your waitress's name at the diner may be Rose; the scent of your car after being detailed might be rose; or the new paint color being suggested to you at the home supply store might be called "rose." The departed are anything but subtle when they want you to notice them. Persistence, repetition, and a little bit of humor are how they make sure you aren't dismissing anything as a mere coincidence when they send you non-literal signs.

Dreams

Have you ever had a dream where a person who has passed visited you? Dreams are often the easiest way for a soul on the other side to contact you, and "dream visitations" can come from loved ones, pets, and people you have known. It's not uncommon, however, to also get these signs from souls you didn't know as well or even at all. You could receive visitations from someone you share a bond with, like the late mother of your good friend, the person who held your job before you, or the previous occupant of your house or apartment.

Visitation dreams have a distinct feel to them. Unlike other dreams, you don't forget them after you wake up, as they feel like real experiences—more like memories than the lingering images of traditional dreams. In these types of dreams, you'll feel like you are having an interaction with the departed as if they are still with you in their physical form. You may see them with a glow or a calming color encircling them, in a white or brightly lit room, or backlit from an unseen yet beautiful light. Light is symbolic of the transformation they have undergone after passing away, and the place where their soul now resides. They may also use emotion to connect with you, sometimes even more than words alone. You might feel their communication rather than "hear" it in your dream. They may use symbols to create layers to their meanings as well. Seeing a phone, text, or voice message in your dream, and perhaps even interacting with it, is usually a metaphor for the distance between your world and the next. Being separated by glass or impermeable yet clear walls is another metaphor they may use to convey the other side. You may also have the sense of visiting places of the past that are significant to them. Being in these spaces, complete with details you thought you had forgotten, and sometimes even smells and other people who have passed are ways a soul can communicate with you while you're asleep.

In twilight moments—the space between being asleep and awake—you may feel a touch or hear a voice of the person on the other side.

Food Smells and Tastes

If you find yourself suddenly compelled to make your late grandmother's famous lasagna or catch a note of the perfume your late mother used to love, it's not just a longing for the past playing tricks with your mind. Those who have crossed over are able to connect with you through your physical senses.

Channeling through your natural clairalience, or "clear smelling" abilities, they can make their presence known via nostalgic smells. The strong scent of coffee when you haven't made a single cup or a whiff of a sweet pine tree when you're miles away from a forest could be the workings of someone trying to get your attention from beyond.

Similar to clairalience, those on the other side can also grab hold of your clairgustance, or "clear tasting" abilities. The sudden urge to make an old family recipe or the random taste of a childhood favorite baked good on your tongue could very well be a loved one connecting with you via your sense of taste. You may find yourself suddenly able to cook a late relative's famous dish from memory alone or feel the need to hunt down a recipe card you know exists. Food and smells from the past are instant connections to those who have passed. Crossing space and time, these senses can instantly transport us directly back to memories of the departed.

With both of these signs, you'll notice that the smell or taste doesn't linger. It tends to come on strongly and disappear soon after without a trace. This can make it easy to brush off as simply a random memory, but the short lifespan of the sign is actually proof that it happened! You can also recreate these smells and tastes for yourself and share them with future generations as a way of connecting with those on the other side.

Noises

Could you have sworn you just heard your departed grandfather's voice or the creaking of his favorite rocking chair? Whispers in your ear, thinking you heard the voice of someone who isn't there, and suddenly noticing a phantom-like song playing in your mind are all ways a soul can make their presence known. Clairaudience, or "clear hearing," is the ability to hear the noises from worlds beyond our own. Those who have crossed over can use this to amplify their own spiritual signs. Thinking you hear a soft chime when there aren't any around or a murmur of a voice when no one is present is simply a way in which the departed is getting your attention. You may also experience a sudden high-pitched ringing in your ears, followed by a buzzing sound. Those who have crossed over will use high-vibrational frequencies to move air and create sound disruptions. When you notice these noises, take a moment to reflect on what you were just thinking about or if there is significance to today's date, or simply keep your mind open for what's to come the rest of the day. More than likely, once the noise gets your attention, you'll begin to see other signs.

Signature Signs

Notice any quirky happenings lately that remind you of a departed loved one's unique personality? While you can connect with and receive signs from anyone who has crossed over, there is a special bond shared with those you loved. When you recall this relationship, it comes to life with its own unique memories and nuances—and these are the very things that your loved one will use when sending you messages from beyond. Their own signature signs will come through to you and will not only remind you of something they said, did, or stood for but will also give you the feeling that their spirit is with you now.

Signature signs are anything that have a unique call back to a loved one. Finding bobby pins everywhere you go and knowing they are from your grandmother who loved her pin curls, finding out your new romantic interest drives the same vintage car as your deceased father, and realizing that your new baby was born on your late grandfather's birthday are all examples of signature signs.

Your loved one has left their physical form, but their soul is intact and wholly available to you. Signature signs can become touchstones you share with these spirits as a means of continuing the relationship after they have passed on.

You can also expect signature signs to infiltrate all other signs that come your way. Those who have crossed over love to put their own spin on the traditional signs explored in Part 2 of this book. Seeing a cardinal and knowing it was your late best friend's favorite bird, smelling the smoke of a favorite uncle's cigar, and repeatedly hearing the favorite song of your late child are all ways in which the ones you love are telling you, "I'm here! I haven't changed in the ways that truly matter."

Where Do I Start?

Asking yourself who you feel sent the sign will be your first step in deciphering it, since each sign's meaning depends on who is using it to communicate. Usually, your first hunch about the sender will be the correct one; listen to your intuition. Hearing a song that reminds you of your late brother, seeing an advertisement with a familiar saying you attribute to a departed friend, and having a feeling that the consistently missing items in your home may be the work of the late previous owner are hunches you can begin to lean into, and eventually trust.

As you get used to reading signs, you'll notice your ability to intuit a sign and understand who sent it and why will get stronger. You may also notice even more signs: The memory, consideration, and attention you give to those on the other side provide them the fuel to send an abundance of signs your way!

Understanding that everything can have more than one meaning, as well as checking in with your own emotional attachment to the sign itself, will also help in deciphering what the other side is trying to communicate. Remember, emotion is an amazing conduit for deeper messages from those who have passed on. Consider the possible meanings and lean into the feelings that come up for you regarding that sign.

As you read more about the following signs and start tracking the ones you receive, feel free to come back to Part 1 whenever needed for a refresher on the types of signs and how you might receive them, or even just a reminder to keep yourself open to messages from those on the other side. Their advice, stories, affirmations, and more are out there, just waiting to be noticed!

PART 2

The Dictionary of Signs

The following signs are some of the most commonly seen and received. Of course, their meanings can vary greatly depending on culture, region, religion, and personal experience, so keeping context in mind and trusting your intuition will help you decipher what you see. Above all, it's important to remember that this is a personal conversation between you and the other side. The cues, emotions, and memories that come up in your interpretations make these messages uniquely your own.

Additionally, this list is anything but complete! While common signs are included here, there are countless ways that those on the other side can make their presence known. And as you continue this journey into signs, you may feel compelled to add new ones to this list, whether in the Signs Log of Part 3, or in a separate notebook or smartphone note. When you tap into the frequency of the other side, those who have crossed over will talk back. Your creativity, open-mindedness, and awareness of your surroundings will be your tools for decoding their language of signs.

Advertisement

A creative reach-out from the other side.

The tendency to notice a TV commercial, a social media-sponsored post, or even a printed flier isn't unusual in daily life. However, when you begin seeing snippets of advertisements that seem to speak directly to you, it is more than just a random coincidence! Those on the other side will use your attention and effectively direct it so that you receive messages via the frequent ads you are already inundated with in your daily life. Be on the lookout for names, significant dates, and special songs and quotes that have meaning to you. You may see a birth date used on an ad for jewelry or a name embroidered across a sweatshirt, or perhaps hear a song that was used at a shared special event.

What to Do: Take a screenshot of these signs when they pop up on your phone or write them down when you see them. The patterns will become more frequent and easier to spot when the departed knows you're on the hunt for all the ways they are trying to get your attention.

Communicating Back: Travel

An adventure with the purpose of spiritual connection strengthens the bond between you and those on the other side. Traveling to a place you know a loved one always wanted to go, or had spent a portion of their lives in, is a meaningful way to soulfully connect. You may also be compelled to base your travels on a person you didn't know yet feel inspired by. Ancestors, relatives, or even those who shared a life's work or a passion similar to your own can be spiritually contacted in this manner. Journeying to a place they lived or worked in unites you in this shared mindspace. When planning your travels, make space for spontaneous side trips or tours, as you may become aware of spiritual messages received en route. Finding a way to leave your own mark while you visit can prolong the correspondence for years to come. Take a similar photo, leave a trinket in an appropriate spot, or invest in the community in some small way to nourish the bond you already share.

Air Movement

An auditory sign asking for immediate attention.

A woosh of air passing by your ears or a sense that your clothes and hair are being moved by unseen forces may not just be a random breeze floating by. Those on the other side have the ability to move the air in your environment in order to get your attention. You may notice papers fluttering off your desk, candle flames acting erratically, or even a temporary rush of air that feels markedly colder. When you feel this sudden and unexplainable air movement, combined with a sense of knowing or even anxiety, you can consider it a spiritual communication. There is someone who wants you to be aware of their soul's presence at this moment.

What to Do: Acknowledge any thoughts about whoever comes to mind in this circumstance. Take a moment to also reflect on any thoughts you were having prior to this occurrence, and any current dilemmas or happenings at the forefront of your thoughts. Chances are there is a soul trying to get in touch and offer their support.

Ant

A tiny symbol of devotion and dedication.

The ant is hardworking and diligent. It supports its fellow ants in a beautiful expression of community and selflessness. Because of this, the ant symbolizes devotion, dedication, persistence, and unwavering focus. Its commitment to the well-being of others and the ways it collaborates with other ants also carry a deep meaning for this creature. When you see this symbol, it is a soul expressing their devoted love to you. You're a part of a much bigger picture, and understanding where you help others and are cared for in return can give you purpose and joy.

What to Do: Think about where you are expressing your own devotion, dedication, and focus in life right now. Reflect on anyone who may share that same devotion with you who is no longer living. Chances are that is the person communicating with you through this sign!

Banyan (Leaf/Tree)

A sign of eternal life and immortality of the soul.

The banyan tree with its unique growth pattern expands infinitely. Since it can live and grow for centuries, it serves in many cultures as a symbol of eternal life and the immortality of the soul. In numerous spiritual traditions, the banyan tree is seen as a way to connect with the divine. Seeing this symbol in your life is a reminder that the soul is eternal and immortal. What fades from the physical realm lives on in another realm. Those who have crossed over want you to take time to connect with the part of your own self, the soul, that will never perish.

What to Do: Invest in the health of your spiritual self today. Set aside a few moments to meditate and sit in nature. Know that your spiritual health is essential and the effort you put in is well spent.

Communicating Back:
Plant a Tree in Their Memory

Planting a tree creates a living legacy for those on the other side. This tribute carries much meaning, not only for those who've crossed over but for those still living. The beauty, longevity, and environmental contribution of the tree is an energy that communicates the importance of that person who has left this world. You may want to choose a tree that has personal significance to the departed and can give generations to come a similar appreciation, such as a lilac tree. You may also choose a tree that symbolically reflects the dedicated work they did in this lifetime. Perhaps you decide to place an oak tree where they raised their large family or plant a magnolia tree where you can enjoy it to recall your everlasting bond. No matter what tree you choose to honor their memory, the thought put into it is what brings their soul closer to your own and allows them to continue their bond with this realm for generations to come.

Bat

A sign pointing a new way forward.

A bat's ability to use echolocation to gracefully navigate through the night sky is the perfect metaphor for finding your own path in life's darkness. When dealing with grief or painful or troubled times, it can be difficult to find your way forward. The bat is a symbol of transformation and the human determination to pull ahead in times of great sorrow. Seeing this symbol is a message from the other side saying, "You are ready to find your way to a new beginning." It is a meaningful sign that encourages you to face your fears in unfamiliar spaces.

What to Do: Take some time to sit with the things in life you'd like to change (for example, a current financial predicament or an unfavorable relationship pattern). Welcome new beginnings with an open heart, knowing that you will be able to navigate unfamiliar territory with the sense of self you have cultivated within.

Bear

A powerful symbol of protection from the other side.

The bear is a strong creature known for its powerful form and protective nature when raising cubs. It is because of this juxtaposition that the bear symbolizes fierce protection, nurturing care, and enduring wisdom. When you see this symbol in your life, a soul is sending you their protection from the other side. Facing trying times can create a feeling of fear and vulnerability, and the departed is letting you know that you aren't alone in these trials. Their memory is a presence you can lean on for strength!

What to Do: Reevaluate some challenging relationships, contexts, and situations that are currently ongoing. It may be a time to refortify some of your boundaries to make sure you are being treated the way you should be.

Bee

A reminder to savor the sweetness of life.

Revered for its hardworking nature, hive teamwork, and impressive talents of pollinating plants and making honey, the bee often represents prosperity, fertility, and generosity. When you repeatedly see this symbol, know that the other side is encouraging you to savor the sweetness of this life. There is much to be enjoyed while on the physical plane, and you are prompted to find joy where you can. Additionally, the bee finds purpose in community and duty, reminding you that happiness is better when it's shared with the ones you love.

What to Do: Make a plan to spend time with the people in your life who support and love you. As you connect with these like-minded souls, feel the gratitude for the ability you have to share joy in life with those you care for most.

Communicating Back: Consider a Tattoo

Tattoos with meaning are a consistent conduit between you and the one who has crossed over. Carefully considering which tattoo to get is a process that those on the other side are often interested in and will frequently give you signs about. Noticing a bee or a certain bird visiting your windowsill every day, frequently encountering a specific symbol, or being drawn to a particular song lyric after they've passed isn't coincidental. This may be the departed giving you suggestions on what to choose for the everlasting reminder of your shared bond.

Beetle

An inspiring message to honor your place in the cycle of life.

The beetle undergoes a metamorphosis throughout its lifetime, demonstrating that change is necessary for survival. It is associated with good luck, rebirth, and the natural cycle of life and death. Seeing this symbol is a message from someone on the other side that they have completed this cycle and are reborn into a new world. They send you comfort and reassurance that all is well in the natural order of things. Seeing your place in this very same cycle can motivate you to make the most of it. This is a sign asking you to connect to your inner strength and wisdom as you undergo the changes necessary to move forward in the world around you.

What to Do: Look within and reflect on your goals for personal growth today. Remember that you are capable of amazing feats and connected to a wisdom that comes from a spiritual source.

Bell

A welcome sign of spiritual communication.

Whether it is from a church steeple or an ornament in your house, the sound of a bell symbolizes purity, protection, and spiritual communication. The ringing of bells can often be associated with a warning or an alert. Reminders on your phone, indications of danger, and wake-up calls all use bell sounds in order to get your attention. However, in a more spiritual sense, the bell is a symbol of the voice of the divine, as it is able to recreate sounds that are on higher vibrations around us. When you hear a bell, know that a soul on the other side is alerting you to their presence and inviting you to feel welcome to continue a correspondence.

What to Do: When you hear a bell ringing out of nowhere or from a known location, check in with your emotions for a sense of who may be communicating with you. You may wish to ring a bell back, inviting this energy to come to you with their messages and signals.

Billboard

A literal "sign" from a spirit.

One favorite way those on the other side like to connect is through street signs, billboards, or shop names that you're passing by, using them to flood you with a feeling of intense recognition. These are literal signs used to grab your attention, and these types of short-form yet powerful messages are usually answering a question you presently have. It's an easy way for the departed to make their presence known. It's important to pay attention and keep an open mind with this type of spiritual signage, as someone on the other side is working quickly and intensely to direct you to where they need you to look. Trusting your own intuition when seeing these types of signs will allow you to know if they are merely coincidental or divinely inspired.

What to Do: Play a fun game with the other side by asking them for a sign today. Keep your mind and eyes open as you move about your day, and consider all the places your attention goes as potential places for communication.

Birch Tree

An encouragement toward new beginnings.

The birch tree is one of the first to grow in land that has been cleared by storm, fire, or humankind. It grows quickly and has a sturdy constitution that provides people with shelter, medicine, and other necessities of life. Because of this, it is often a symbol of new beginnings, shelter, and protection. The birch tree survives harsh conditions, and seeing this symbol in your life suggests that you too have weathered many storms. A departed soul is sending you this sign to nudge you toward a new beginning, one that may seem frightening but is in your best interest. The other side believes in your ability to start anew.

What to Do: Consider a place in your life where you could use a fresh start, like a geographical move or a reboot in a health-related routine. Think about how a new beginning in this area will allow you to have more freedom to be who you are.

Bluebird

A symbolic sending of good luck.

Your happiness is a precious thing, and someone on the other side is making their presence known to you so that you prioritize that happiness today! The bluebird is a sign of contentment, joy, and celebration. It serves to remind you to enjoy life and to do what you need to do to feel good in this present moment. In many cultures the bluebird symbolizes good luck, new possibilities, and companionship. When you see this sign, know that you are being sent some good fortune. There will be reason to celebrate, and you'll know that the energy of the spirit realm is with you while you do so.

What to Do: Keep your eyes open for some good luck today, like an easy commute to work, a friend offering you a helping hand, or awareness of a problem before it became much worse. When you receive this luck, celebrate life in a way that makes you feel joy. Walk outside barefoot, eat a sweet treat, or sing along to a few of your favorite songs. Spiritual energy connects to you while you enjoy this moment of good fortune.

Book Passages

Spiritual signal to pay close attention.

The overwhelming flood of emotion that comes with reading a particular passage or quote in a book, or even spotting a certain book title, is more than a mood swing; it's your soul's recognition of a message being directed to you. Those on the other side can direct you to passages, quotes, and other forms of printed media in order to communicate with you. They also have an ability to influence the environment to make sure that these types of messages are apparent where they know you'll be looking. When you see these particular written signs, a soul is asking you to pay even more close attention to your environment. Chances are the spirit realm is just getting started.

What to Do: Make sure you bookmark or screenshot what resonated with you so deeply. Keep it close to you for future reference and as a touchstone for future connections with the other side.

Book Titles

Book titles with special meaning are a way in which those who cross over can alert you to their presence. While strolling through a bookstore, you are in the perfect mental space to receive these not-so-subtle signs. Noticing a particular title repeatedly, seeing book titles that were the departed's favorite, or even spotting titles that seem to be giving you some advice and direction you would have gotten from that soul is an example of this phenomenon. When this happens, check your own intuition and personal knowledge of the one who has crossed to decode this sign. You may be receiving it as a way of remembrance, or you could be directed to dive a bit deeper in your communications. You may want to pick up this book to read and see what more comes out of your interaction with the text.

Bridge

A reassuring sign of your connection.

Seeing a bridge and suddenly feeling a sense of peace, tranquility, or longing is more than just admiration of beautiful architecture. Bridges convey a sense of transition and often symbolize the journey between this world and the next. They are associated with overcoming one's own obstacles and represent progress. They signify hope, transformation, and the sense of adventure one needs to cultivate. When you see this symbol, know that the other side is sending you a reassuring sign of the continued connection you share. The transitions between phases in this present lifetime will always be supported by someone on the other side.

What to Do: Consider where in your life you are making a change or going through a significant transformation. Rest in the knowledge that you are spiritually connected and supported at this time.

Butterfly

A sign of soulful company.

The butterfly is often associated with joy, transformation, and the rebirth of the soul. It is a metaphor for hope and bravery, as it inspires people to go forth always into the unknown. Undergoing its own metamorphosis from caterpillar to its winged state, the butterfly represent the soul's freedom in the afterlife. It is a sign that those on the other side can send to reiterate the eternal life of the soul. When you see a butterfly, know that a soulful presence is saying, "I am with you now and forever."

What to Do: When seeing this symbol, think immediately about who could be contacting you. Send out your own message of gratitude and sit for a few moments in their spiritual company.

Communicating Back: Choose a Sign

It's possible you don't always feel like you are receiving signs. Some souls may feel a little quieter, or you might worry you have been missing their messages. Choosing a sign specifically for the departed can become a touchstone for cross communication. Designate a flower, animal, or some other natural sign as your new signal of spiritual correspondence. Now, simply pay attention to your surroundings! No matter how small or coincidental the signs appear to be at first, always give gratitude to the person you designated this sign to.

Cardinal

A classic, bright red sign of presence and love.

Seeing the striking red color of the cardinal as it visits you in your yard, appears in art, or flutters past you while on a walk is a soul's special way of saying, "I am with you now." The cardinal has long embodied spiritual significance as its red feathers carry various meanings of love, protection, and devotion. It is believed to carry messages of the divine from one world to the next. Receiving this sign can be considered a direct correspondence between you and someone who has crossed over. A cardinal visiting you by your window is especially meaningful, as this symbolizes the separation between the physical world and the spiritual one.

What to Do: When you see a cardinal, take a moment to fill your heart with the renewed hope that comes when experiencing a spiritual presence.

Carnation

A floral sign of devotion and unconditional love.

The carnation flower carries a meaning of devoted love. Additionally, its unique shape has led it to be symbolic of distinction and fascination. The carnation represents the special bond you share with someone on the other side. The appearance of this sign can be seen as a reflection of gratitude and appreciation from the other side to you. When you repeatedly see the flower or its artistic depictions in your daily life, know that a soul on the other side is saying, "I am devoted to you." They acknowledge that although they aren't here in the physical world, the bond you share is eternal.

What to Do: Take a moment to sit and consider how special and unique the bond is that you share with someone on the other side. As the emotions flow, feel their spiritual presence surrounding you.

Flower Sign

Just like those who have crossed over, you can also use flowers to communicate across realms. Choose a flower you feel especially fond of or one that you associate with the departed. Talk to this person in your mind and ask them to send you this flower in many ways—for example, receiving a card with the flower's depiction or seeing wreaths using this exact flower everywhere you go. You may also want to initiate this exchange by planting this flower in your garden or finding artistic renditions of the flower to use as decor.

Cat

**A spiritual indication that you are
communicating beyond this realm.**

Looking into a cat's eyes, it's easy to see why they are often
thought of as a bridge between the physical world and the
spiritual world—a messenger from one plane to the next. The
cat, with its mysterious and independent behavior, symbolizes
wisdom, curiosity, and patience. When you see a cat showing
up on your doorstep after someone has passed, or in constant
symbols being sent your way, know that someone on the other
side is confirming your inner ability to communicate with them
still. The way in which the cat displays balance is a metaphor
for your own capabilities of living in this physical world while
always connecting to the unseen.

What to Do: When you see this symbol show up in your life,
it's time to start listening to your intuition! The hunches you get,
feelings you absorb, and thoughts you have aren't as happenstance as you may have previously assumed. Take time to consider which of these may be messages from those who have
crossed over.

Caterpillar

A message of fortitude, patience, and hidden potential.

The caterpillar waits patiently for its metamorphosis to occur. Its seemingly unremarkable appearance falls away to eventually be born again into a new and transformed creature. Because of this, the caterpillar symbolizes fortitude, patience, and one's hidden potential. When you see this symbol, know that a soul on the other side is reminding you of your own talents and encouraging you to tap into the strengths they have always seen in you. Just as the caterpillar diligently spins its cocoon and prepares for great and unknown changes, you too can begin to lean into your own inner wisdom and allow for amazing things to happen.

What to Do: Think about where you've been feeling impatient lately. There are most likely a few spots in life where you aren't being seen or supported by those in the physical world. But you have the support of those on the other side to make sure you create the best space for yourself to thrive. You have wonderful things coming your way!

Cherry Blossom

A beautiful symbol of impermanence.

The delicate, pink cherry blossom gracing onlookers with its presence every spring brings many meanings. Its aesthetic beauty reminds you of the impermanence of life, beauty, and youth. The cherry blossom has long been a symbol of the cycle of life, as each stage of its blossoming, fruiting, and flourishing ties into themes of birth, growth, and renewal. When finding yourself faced with this symbol, know that you are receiving a sign that lovingly reminds you of the impermanence of cycles in life. The cycle you are in now has an important purpose, and whether it feels difficult or incredibly joyful, it is temporary.

What to Do: Reflect on the cycle of life you are in now and how it serves your greater purpose. Try to capture this stage in life so you can revisit it in the future: Write a journal entry, take a photo, or draw a picture of whatever it is that captures the emotion of this moment.

Chime

A musical sign for remembrance.

The phantom sound of glass or metal sweetly clinking is perhaps not just your mind playing tricks on you, or even an actual chime ringing nearby. The chime is thought to neutralize energy, bring in positive thoughts, and provide context for clarity. Hearing a chiming sound that isn't physically there is a message of spiritual communication. Clairaudience is the ability to psychically "hear" sounds from other realms. Those who have crossed over can use this skill you inherently have to give you their messages and inspirations, and they are doing so now.

What to Do: When you hear a chiming sound regularly, it is the departed's way of saying, "I remember you." Take the time to sit with your own emotions when you hear this, knowing that you are never forgotten.

Communicating Back: Hang Chimes

The sound of chimes energetically purifies the environment and creates the perfect context for spiritual communication. Purposefully placing them with this intention will further help souls send more signs and even at times manipulate the chimes themselves. You may notice the chimes moving when there is no wind or an uptick in chime-like noises without any movement from them at all. Decorating with chimes is a little way to set up a sounding system for you and the departed.

Chrysanthemum

A floral reminder of rebirth, happiness, and memory.

Life is a cycle, an endless loop. What those in this physical realm call "death" can be interpreted as "rebirth" in a spiritual sense. From the perspective of those who have passed, they have been reborn into an eternal realm. If you are seeing the chrysanthemum repeatedly, either in its physical form or in artistic depictions, you can take it as a message from the other side that there is more to this world after you leave its physical stage. While the pain of loss—the grief and challenges that come with it—is real in this life, seeing this flower is a little nudge from the other side that someday you'll meet those you miss once again.

What to Do: When seeing the chrysanthemum, take a moment to happily remember the one you miss so dearly. Reflect on how their presence in your life was a blessing. Tell a close friend or family member a story or two about this departed person to honor their memory.

Cicada

An indication that change is imminent.

Emerging from underground after many years, the cicada demonstrates that life is a cyclical journey. After experiencing loss, the time it takes to work through the grief and sorrow can feel like a waking slumber. The surrounding world seems to go on while you stand in a numb state. The cicada symbolizes rebirth, the cycles of life and death, and the indication that change is in the immediate future. When you see this symbol, you can interpret it as an alert from the other side that it's time to wake up once again. Your rest is over and the world is ready for you to reemerge and live freely.

What to Do: Reflect on ways you can embrace the journey of life. Think about where you could use some change and how it would benefit you. Perhaps you need to revitalize your social relationships to connect soulfully, or clean out an area of your home where unnecessary clutter has affected your ability to live and think clearly. Look excitedly toward the future as you anticipate new challenges, opportunities, and inspired moments to come.

Clock

A spiritual reminder that time is a limited resource.

If you find yourself drawn to the rhythmic ticking of a clock, or you are seeing clock imagery in all aspects of your life, it's more than just your attention to the time of day! The clock represents the fleeting life humans experience on this earthly plane. It is a symbol of mortality, the cycle of life, and order and punctuality. Your time here is finite, and those on the other side know this truth all too well. You are seeing this symbol as a reminder that your time is a limited resource, and you are allowed to make the most of it. Wasting your time in places that no longer serve you or in relationships that aren't beneficial is no longer an option. You have important things to do—things that are prioritized when you truly acknowledge and understand the concept of the passage of time.

What to Do: Make a mental list of all the items on your to-do list today. Think about where you can cut something out that is simply a waste of your time. Replace that item with something that feels good to you.

Set Your Own Clock

Dedicating an analog clock to a certain time of day, every day, is a creative way to call in spiritual energy. Setting a clock to a specific time that correlates to a meaningful number will also help in bringing the frequency of that intention forward. For example, keeping a clock on 5:18 to commemorate your late grandmother's birthday of May 18, or on 12:08 as an homage to the address of a home that was significant to the departed's memory, is a way to call their attention strongly to you. You may want to keep this clock in a sacred area of your home such as a meditation space, a cozy nook, or anywhere you can fondly and repeatedly see it throughout the day.

Cloud

A spiritual tool for abstract communication.

Gazing up at the sky and seeing an image that immediately resonates with you isn't just your imagination running wild. Spirits use clouds to communicate with you. Seeing a shape that resembles your beloved cat from childhood, a loved one's face, or even a symbol you find meaningful imprinted in a cloud floating by can create a surge of emotion. The ways in which you see the images, along with the feelings experienced before and after, will give you further information on who is speaking with you and what they are saying. Regardless of the message, the feeling of being contacted is a gift that fills the heart.

What to Do: Quickly draw the image you saw in the cloud(s). Reflect on this image and what overall sentiment feels most aligned to you.

Coat of Arms

A signal of ancestral interest.

The coat of arms represents generosity, legacy, and bravery. When you begin to take special interest in this symbol or find yourself confronted with many coats of arms that catch your attention, you are receiving a signal from ancestors on the other side. These may be your direct ancestors, or ancestors that have connected to you via a project, passion, or work you presently have. The coat of arms is about memory—exactly what is necessary for spirits to be able to send signs. The sacrifice of those who came before you is evident in all you have today in the present moment. They are asking you to preserve this memory so that future generations continue to connect with and make the most of the lasting legacy they've left behind.

What to Do: Look into this ancestral heritage in great detail. Follow any curiosities, insights, or leads you may receive.

Communicating Back: Create a Family History

Ancestors on the other side appreciate recognition from the generations they never met in the physical realm. Organizing, creating, and updating family genealogy history for all family members to have access to is a powerful way to make contact with ancestral energy. When those on the other side have the vibration of memory to tap into, they can send you messages, support, and love.

Cocoon

A mindful message about divine timing.

The weight of feeling stuck, without direction or purpose, can be scary. When seeing the symbol of the cocoon, however, you are receiving a mindful message from a spirit that you may simply be in a metamorphosis stage. The cocoon signifies transformation, rebirth, and the timing of the divine. Just like the caterpillar enters its cocoon in order to pause and transform, you too are undergoing significant change. You are being sent a message from a soulful presence that you aren't stuck; you're altering your entire life. When the divine timing is right, this cocoon phase will fall away and the next chapter of your beautiful life will begin.

What to Do: Consider how you can change your perspective on this present phase of life. Think about where you feel stuck and reflect on how you've actually been mindfully and spiritually changing the entire time.

Coffee

An alert to notice a spiritual influence today.

Phantom smells are a common way for souls to get your attention. Using your already existing clairalience, or ability to psychically "smell," those on the other side will send messages. Coffee symbolizes opportunity, the need to be alert, and the awakening of the spiritual self. When you smell this scent but no actual coffee is in sight, know that the departed is giving you a message of their presence. You may associate this smell with a specific loved one on the other side, or consider it loving advice to stay attuned to more signs to come.

What to Do: When you smell this sign, take a moment to feel grateful for the love that is coming through to you from the other side. Be more aware of your surroundings today as you search for the reasons why this spirit is advising you to stay alert.

Communicating Back: Prepare Traditional Dishes

The dishes the departed thoughtfully put together have meaning. Perhaps your late grandmother had a pie she was famous for making, or a coworker made a soup that seemed to cure any ailment. Creating a signature dish that you associate with someone who is now on the other side is a way to connect and communicate with them. If possible, track down the exact recipe, including the cookware they used, so you can experience the bond between realms in a more profound way.

Coin

A message of self-worth.

Finding a coin isn't necessarily an uncommon occurrence. It also happens to be a convenient way for the departed to send you messages. Coins allow souls to send a message of abundance, self-worth, and their continued support of you while they are on the other side. Taking notice of where you find coins, as well as in which circumstances, will allow you to decipher between the insignificant and the meaningful. Perhaps you always find coins while you're in transit, in the bottom of your shoe, or around the door to your home. Notice the details on the coins as well. Perhaps certain years on the coins hold significance, or the way in which the coins are lying is patterned or consistent. Also note the coin combinations—it could be that adding the change up always leads to a significant number, the same types of coins are found next to one another, or you always find them heads up. In these patterns, you'll find messages that resonate, as well as a sense of the other side.

What to Do: Be on the lookout for patterns with your coin findings. Send a silent thought of love and gratitude to the one(s) who you feel sent these signs.

Communicating Back: Start a Coin Jar

The coins you've been finding from those who have crossed over can be kept and stored as a way to communicate with those on the other side and keep their memory close to you. You may want to allocate a meaningful container for these coins, such as in a cup or vase the departed particularly enjoyed. Decorating a jar in a way that reminds you of them is another way to put your own spin on this correspondence. Place the jar in a place of honor and remember the effort the departed went through to keep reminding you of their eternal presence.

Crane

An ancient symbol of inner wisdom.

There is an inner wisdom within you that is eternal and abundant. Of course, it can be hard to trust what you see and think when difficult times create an imbalance in your mindset, emotions, and daily life. The sign of a crane is a call for a focused look inward for the answers you seek. The crane is a significant symbol in numerous cultures and is associated with wisdom, longevity, and creativity. It can also represent loving advice and the arrival of joyous times.

What to Do: When seeing this symbol, ask yourself in what ways you could keep your own counsel. Perhaps there have been too many advice-givers muddying the waters of your mind with their well-intended suggestions. Think of a way you could answer a question you've been asking yourself on your own.

Crow

**Confirmation that messages are received
between this world and the next.**

There is a world that cannot be seen with physical eyes, yet it is real. The crow is a symbol of interworld connectedness as it is thought to be a messenger from one world to the next. When you are confronted with the imagery of the crow, know that your own spiritual intuition can be trusted. Your messages to the other side have been received and seen by keen and intelligent energy. The crow has long been associated with guidance, one's psychic abilities, and overall protection. When you see this sign repeatedly, know that a spiritual source is saying to you, "I hear you, I see you, and you are safe."

What to Do: Your intuition is a guide, and this symbol is asking you to tune into it more closely. Sit with your inner voice and start listening to it before any other voices. When you feel spiritual energy around you, believe it!

Daffodil

A floral symbol signaling your ability to rise again.

After a cold, hard winter, the daffodil rises from the frozen ground to give the world its hopeful beauty. It is often the first burst of color you can see after a dark, frigid season. The daffodil gives a feeling of new beginnings and serves as a reminder of the beautiful things that await you in life. This flower is often associated with joy, positivity, and healing. Seeing it either in its physical form or as an artistic depiction many times over is a message to renew your perspective toward hope. The ability the daffodil has to transform itself, survive, and rise again is the symbolic advice you are receiving from a spiritual source.

What to Do: When seeing the daffodil in your life, think of ways you can shift your perspective toward hope moving forward. Think of ways you've been strong throughout your grief. You, like the daffodil, are rising again after a difficult time.

Daisy

Spiritual permission to feel happy.

The darkness that can follow a person in grief can seem impenetrable. Seeing a daisy is a sign from a soulful energy to take joy where and when you can. The daisy has long been a symbol of innocence, purity, and simplicity. After loss, it can feel like a betrayal to feel gratitude or chase any sort of happiness. This flower is your permission from those on the other side to feel cheerful once again, even if it's in the smallest way at first. Connecting with your joy is a beautiful way to honor those who have passed on.

What to Do: Take a moment to list a few things that give you simple gratitude. The first sip of coffee in the morning, the feeling of sun on your face, and the comfort of a blanket wrapped around you are all little ways to soak in tiny amounts of joy wherever you can.

Date (Calendar)

A specific symbol of memory and remembrance.

Noticing that your new job begins on your late father's birthday, or that your due date happens to be the day your brother passed, may not be a simple coincidence! Calendar dates have special meaning to those on the other side, and they can send you these dates as signs not only of remembrance, but also to offer some validation that they are lending you their support. The numbers of the dates themselves may be showing up in your life quite often. For example, you may see a specific date that's meaningful to you—such as your late grandparents' anniversary—show up in numeric form on paperwork, receipts, room numbers, or anywhere else over and over again. A loved one on the other side is saying, "I remember you; do you remember me too?"

What to Do: These are happy signals from a departed loved one, and when you see them, take note of how you immediately feel. It can be emotional to connect your loved one with the date they are sending you, but when you do, you are acknowledging their participation in your life, even after they've crossed over.

Pay Attention to the Calendar

If you are noticing more signs on a certain day, make sure to double-check your calendar. Significant dates hold more power for souls on the other side to come through and make their presence known. Special birthdays, anniversaries, and even dates of their passing can amplify their energy. You may notice that your baby's due date, a closing date for your new home, or a date of a graduation is one that has significance to the departed. You can take advantage of these dates as well. Planning the grand opening of your new business or simply setting aside time to reflect on a date that has meaning brings your bond closer. As always, attention is a magnet for spiritual activity. Notice the signs that pop up when you are being extra mindful on these special dates.

Deer

Affirmation of your spiritual connection.

The elegance and grace of the deer have inspired people throughout time and across different cultures. Its very essence seems to evoke a tranquility that everyone desires. The deer symbolizes protection, intuition, and one's own spiritual connection. It is seen as a sign of good luck and a carrier of spirit messages from beyond. The deer also represents inner wisdom and your ability to navigate through the unknown. When you see this symbol, know that a soulful energy is saying, "I am here with you." You aren't alone because your strong spiritual connection is always providing a pathway to those on the other side. Looking within and feeling their devotion is all you have to do to know they are reaching out to you now.

What to Do: Sit and feel the reassurance that spiritual energy is communicating with you. Trust the signs, feelings, and inner wisdom you receive at this time: Nothing is random!

Dog

A special sign of loyalty, love, and devotion.

Confronting the loss of someone includes grieving how they made you feel, and all the amazing words and actions that showed their commitment to you. The dog is symbolic of loyalty, love, and devotion. It is often seen as a wise spiritual teacher as well as a protector. When you see this symbol, know that you are receiving a special message of allegiance and support from a soul on the other side. Although the physical world no longer holds them here, they are coming through to you now in the spirit of admiration.

What to Do: When you see this sign, tap into your own self-confidence and power. You are a wonderful person worthy of love and friendship. Reflect on times when the departed made you feel their care and devotion.

Communicating Back: Name a Pet in Their Honor

Animals are natural conduits between this world and the next. One special way you can let someone know you are remembering them is by giving a new pet a meaningful name. Naming a pet after a loved one, a mutual interest you shared, or even an inside joke between you is a lighthearted yet loving way to keep their energy close by. You can call in the energy of someone you weren't as familiar with through this act as well, naming a pet after an ancestor you wish you had known, or a member of the community you are inspired by.

Dolphin

Validation of the soul's freedom.

The dolphin is amazing with its clever, playful nature and how gracefully it moves through oceans. Carrying many meanings, it is a symbol for spiritual guidance, joy, and the soul's freedom. The dolphin has long been seen as a bridge between this world and the next. The departed sends you this symbol to let you know that their soul is unbounded by the constraints of the physical body. They are able to move about playfully now with new unconstrained joy, just as the dolphin does in its underwater playground. Seeing this symbol is a validation that someone who has passed on is safe and thriving on the other side.

What to Do: Reflect on what you may need to do to feel free in your own life today. Think about places you feel constrained and held back, and what you can do to unchain yourself. The inspiration of the soul's freedom isn't just for the afterlife; it's for you too!

Dove

A peaceful symbol of connection.

The dove comforts many in their deepest sorrows and inspires a feeling of hope. It seems to transverse this realm to the next, reminding people that what separates them from each other is only material. The spiritual symbolism of the dove is a cross-cultural and time-enduring theme of love and connection. Seeing this bird is a clear message that a soulful energy is present and your bond with them is intact. When you see a dove, know that the departed is saying, "You can connect with me at any time."

What to Do: Connect with those on the other side in some small way today. For example, you can send out a prayer of connection, or light a candle in honor of someone who has crossed over. Whatever you choose to do, know it is received wholeheartedly!

Consider the Cultural Context

Ancestry can play a deciding role in what the signs are saying. Doing some research into your ancestral, cultural, and geographic traditions shapes the meanings of the symbols that are sent to you from the other side. While many signs have universal meanings, consider the deeper and layered nuances that have originated through sacred religious ceremonies, cultural heritages, and ancestral histories for more context into what each sign means. Those on the other side will tap into their own traditions in order to send signs your way.

Dragonfly

A reassuring symbol of enduring wisdom.

The dragonfly is an enduring symbol with many meanings. It represents wisdom, change, and a connection to the elemental world, as it can live (and thrive) in different habitats. The dragonfly often signifies the versatility of the human spirit, and the changes one can undergo with grace and adaptability. When considering such a big change as death, it's frightening to think that all you do, say, and have learned will be gone with you forever. The dragonfly symbol is being sent your way as a message of enduring wisdom. A soulful energy is saying, "My wisdom lives in you now." The memories, lessons, and teachings the departed pass on are a gift that never dies, and those on the other side recognize and connect with that wisdom still.

What to Do: Ponder the lessons you learned from someone who has crossed over. Create a plan for how you can pass this wisdom to others who need it. Giving advice, writing down sentiments, and making sure a legacy is secure are all ways to honor the departed's wisdom.

Duck

A loving message to take care of yourself.

Dipping in and out of small ponds and massive oceans alike, the duck is skilled at staying afloat. This bird has many meanings across cultures; throughout time, it's often associated with balance, perspective, and the strong bonds that support you in life. Repeatedly encountering this symbol is a message from those on the other side asking you to take care of yourself. Your physical, mental, and spiritual selves are all connected, and even from beyond this realm, you are cared for and thought of often.

What to Do: Ask yourself where in your life you could use a little more self-care. Take a nap, see what you can say no to, and perhaps cook yourself a nice meal today. Recognizing where you could use a little TLC and giving that energy to yourself is an act of self-love you deserve—and one those on the other side are asking you to prioritize.

Eagle

A request for a shift in perspective.

As the eagle looks down from its aerial realms, it has expert awareness of how important perspective is—how it changes one's strategy and overall approach to the world. The eagle symbolizes courage, freedom, and deep spiritual connection, as well as the ability to see things in a different way. When you see the eagle, you are being sent a message to change your viewpoint on something. Just because you can't see something now doesn't mean it doesn't exist in a different lens. Spiritual energy is asking you to courageously open your mind and eyes in a new way. There is much freedom to be found when you do!

What to Do: Reflect on a belief or viewpoint you have that could use a different perspective. Is a regret you hold actually a valued life lesson? Or can you reflect upon a rift in a relationship with a renewed empathic lens? Ponder how seeing things differently allows you to navigate your world with more spiritual connection.

Ears Popping

An alert to spiritual frequencies.

When someone on the other side enters your earthly plane with their spiritual energy, they alter the air pressure immediately around you. Feeling your ears fill or pop, or a pressure you normally associate with a change in atmospheric pressure, is a sign that a departed soul is paying you a visit. Ear popping can be a sign of your own soul's ascension, as being able to notice this type of sign requires advanced clairaudient, or "clear hearing," abilities. Your ears can pick up on some higher frequencies that many people are less sensitive to.

What to Do: Practice your clairaudient skills by sitting in nature and noting the sounds all around you. See if you can "hear," or re-create, the sounds later in your mind when you have left this setting.

Communicating Back: Do a Legacy Project

Engraving the departed's name in stone, on a plaque, or in another form and setting it in a space where happy memories are made is a sentimental way to communicate with the other side. Memory is a powerful conduit, and sharing that memory with others through legacy projects is one way to make it last. Choose a legacy brick to be a part of a park pathway, jumpstart a fundraiser for building a few free-standing libraries in their honor, or champion for a public pavilion in their name for all to enjoy.

Electricity

A sign of greeting and familiarity.

TVs randomly switching channels, your electric alarm clock going off without being turned on, or seeing a light turn on suddenly isn't meant to scare you. Rather, it is a friendly sign of greeting from a soul on the other side. When those who have crossed over come through, much of their new bodies in the physical world is energy. They can interact with electronics via this energy to grab your attention and relay a comforting message of presence. They want you to know that life didn't end when they died; it simply continued in a new way.

What to Do: Consider who would be sending you this message. Notice if there are any ties to the departed you would associate with the particular electronic in question, the room it is operating in, or even the time of day, and why. Was it grandpa's favorite channel the TV keeps turning to? Or an alarm sounding at the time of death of a beloved friend? The departed most likely chose their timing and device for a reason!

Electronics Malfunctioning

A validating message of a nearby soul.

If you are noticing your electronics malfunctioning or breaking, think about who may be sending you a sign from the other side before running to a repair shop! Your phone always draining its battery, a certain lightbulb exploding above your head, and security cameras going dark for no apparent reason can be signs from someone on the other side. These types of forceful electronic malfunctions are the result of a soul who is coming through with a strong amount of energy. The ones who've crossed over with big, passionate, and feisty personalities tend to be the ones breaking things when they want to just say hello to you.

What to Do: Take a moment when a seemingly random electronic malfunction happens and think of who might be sending you a message. Feel their presence with you and, just as you would in life, calm them down a bit with some validating words of your own. Saying, "I know you're here and I appreciate you," can settle the energy and allow the connection to continue in a less abrasive way.

Elephant

An acknowledgment of your strength.

The proud and strong elephant is also a gentle and wise animal. Beyond just finding its force inspiring, people can relate to the elephant's family bonds. And because of these traits, the elephant is often a symbol of stability, endurance, and protection. Enduring heartbreak after loss is a test of one's fortitude. Seeing this symbol is a message from the departed acknowledging your inner strength in trying times. When you see this sign, a soulful energy is validating your hard and long journey in life, applauding the discipline and perseverance it took to get you here.

What to Do: Think about ways you can rest today. You have been strong for a long time, but are there offers of help you've been declining that could be beneficial? Create a plan for yourself to get some rest and allow others to help you when they are willing.

Elm (Leaf/Tree)

A spiritual sign of appreciation for your resilience.

The elm tree stands sturdy and tall, its canopy attracting many creatures who make their homes within. This tree is a symbol of strength, resilience, and the unity of community; encountering this sign (either a full elm tree or a leaf/leaves) is a spiritual message of appreciation for your own resilience during a challenging time. You have been a pillar of strength for others to count on, and because of this, your family, friends, and perhaps even community have endured. In a time when the people who need one another most could have drifted apart, you've been the one to hold them together. It hasn't gone unnoticed by someone who appreciates you on the other side.

What to Do: Reflect on how you have made a difficult time a bit easier for those around you, as well as how you've sup-ported others who've needed you. Rest in the knowledge that a soul who has crossed over feels very grateful for you.

Email

A creative electronic greeting.

In the present day, receiving spam emails isn't anything to get too worked up over. Still, this common occurrence can suddenly become a sign when the emails are sent by an address from someone no longer alive, or if the emails have a certain eerie connotation you can't ignore. Notice emails sent with no subject or body, but come from someone you know who has passed, such as a loved one, coworker, or distant relative. Also, take note of emails coming through that have links to you for other reasons, such as projects you're working on or an endeavor you are passionate about. Those on the other side who you may not have known in life, yet share your interests, can use emails to encourage you. Thinking about how you feel, what is going on in your life presently, and further signs you may be getting can help you piece together a larger pattern of what is being communicated from the other side.

What to Do: Sit quietly and focus on the sender of this message. Ask them to send another sign to confirm your connection and the fact that they are communicating with you. Trust what you see next and give this sender your gratitude.

Communicating Back:
Memorialize Their Social Media

A virtual place for people to remember someone who has crossed over is a powerful conduit to their spiritual presence. Memorializing a social media page they once owned, or creating a new one in their honor, allows more bonds to thrive between this realm and the next. You may wish to do this for a person you loved, a figure in the community you were familiar with, or even a stranger who you've learned the story of and feel a deep connection to. You may want to include a space for guests to share stories and post photos, and annually commemorate their birth date or even death date. As the creator of the page, you may find yourself inspired to add history, pictures, and anecdotes you collect along the way. Notice any new ambitions you have toward projects you previously did not connect to, such as an environmental cause they supported or a piece of local history they took pride in preserving. Even though you are the one running the account, the departed can have suggestions they won't shy away from giving you! Prepare to meet new people who add additional narrative to the memory or find yourself invited to events and social circles that give you an opportunity to continue their work in the physical realm.

Fairy Ring

A sign of portals and otherworldly realms.

Naturally occurring circular formations—think mushrooms in your garden, a public park, a wooded path you are walking, etc.—all have spiritual significance. Known as a "fairy ring," this circumstance has long fascinated people, sparking mystery and wonder. It's thought to be a portal to other realms. When you see a fairy ring, a soul is reminding you that they aren't far away, just in a different plane of existence.

What to Do: Sit outside the fairy ring and close your eyes. Connect with your own intuition and emotion and allow yourself to feel settled as you tap into the peace of nature. Many people believe that you can use your clairaudience, or clear hearing, to "hear" the other plane of existence while sitting this way beside a fairy ring.

Feather

A gesture of advice, reassurance, and love.

The feather has long been thought of as a message of peace, spiritual connection, and prayers answered. From your loved one on the other side, it is a strong reminder that they know how much you miss them and are returning the sentiment. A white feather is an even more specific sign that someone who has recently passed has crossed over. Other feather colors have distinct meanings too: A black feather means you are protected, a gray feather means you need to stay focused on peace, a brown feather means you need to ground yourself, and a blue feather means you need to stay spiritually connected.

What to Do: When you see a feather during your day, think of the first person who comes to mind, and consider this a gesture of reassurance and love they are sending to you. If possible, collect the feather as a keepsake!

Traditions

Suddenly getting invited to cultural or religious events that were important to the departed, becoming employed in a space that honors a certain heritage, or noticing an uptick in people entering your life who hold similar celebrations as someone who has crossed over isn't always just a coincidence. Souls on the other side will bring you into traditional mindsets that were paramount in their own lives in order to connect with you.

Fir (Leaf/Tree)

A promise of prosperity.

The evergreen fir tree is the epitome of durability. Known for its resilient nature, the evergreen fir tree has appealed to humans for its various practical uses, including construction and aromatherapy, and it has also held various symbolic meanings throughout time. The fir tree symbolizes prosperity, hope, and new life. It's been used in seasonal ceremonies in numerous cultures, as it also represents enduring inner strength throughout times of transition. When you encounter this symbol, know that a spiritual source is promising you a time of prosperity in the future. You've weathered the storms life has sent your way and braved dark times. You are ready to feel the light of hope and new life again.

What to Do: Buy fir tree essential oil, candles, or sprays to fill your living space with its fresh scent. As you breathe in the smell of the fir tree, you are receiving the sentiment of the soulful energy who is sending this prosperous message your way.

Firefly

A spiritual directive to find your inner light.

With its incredible gift of illuminating the darkness, it's no wonder why the firefly draws such inspiration. It symbolizes hope, rebirth, and the transformation of one's soul. It is associated with self-discovery as well as creative visions. Seeing this symbol is a message for you to find the essence of who you are and to let your inner light shine brightly. It can be overwhelming to climb out of the darkness that comes with life's losses. The firefly is an encouraging message for you to look within and feel faith in your own ability to soulfully shine in the shadows. There is a journey of self-discovery to be had, and you are being nudged along this path.

What to Do: Ponder where you have been feeling your inner light dim lately. Explore ways of connecting to yourself, such as through creative endeavors, talking to a close friend, or beginning a daily journal routine to get your soul awakened once again.

Fish

An indicator of divine intervention.

Since ancient times, the fish has held various meanings and interpretations; it often serves as a symbol of hope and rebirth, of optimism and of intuition. The sight of fish swimming in water in their protective schools gives a sense of security, safety, and preservation. When you see this symbol, a soulful energy is saying, "You are receiving divine intervention." There is a need for you to receive help from the other side at this time. All you have to do is accept it and give thanks for the energy being guided your way!

What to Do: Reflect on the present circumstances in your life. If there is anything you seem to be fighting against that may be better left alone, consider letting it go. It could be a continued intervention in a tumultuous relationship or a push for a project to move forward, which isn't in your best interest. The forces at play around you may be attempting to settle on their own what doesn't serve you.

Flamingo

A celebration of the uniqueness of you.

The colorful hues of the flamingo attract attention and admiration. This bird symbolizes harmony, grace, and emotional connection. Its rare beauty and unique colors make it a natural magnet of wonder. When you see this bird, it's a message from the other side that you too attract unique attention and that you need to make the most of that ability. Being in the spotlight can be uncomfortable, but when you receive the admiration of others, you are giving them the gift of your authentic self. The person you are is the one you are being encouraged to show others.

What to Do: Reflect on some ways you are dimming your own light and hiding who you are from the world. Think of how you can shine just by being who you are. Wear that brightly colored shirt you love, don't shy away from a story you want to tell, or simply laugh out loud when you find something funny. Being you is a gift to everyone you meet!

Footprints

A sign of impermanence, life purpose, and lasting love.

Footprints in the snow, etched in clay, or imprinted in sand can fill people with wonder. Their ephemeral forms mirror much of this life, the impermanent patterns serving as temporary markers of where you have been. Footprints represent your life purpose, your path, and the passage of time. The natural desire to make your mark in the physical realm is challenged by the realization that nothing is permanent. Seeing footprint signs is a reminder from a spiritual energy that the only lasting mark you truly make is on the hearts of those you love and care about. When you see this sign, know that a soul is remembering the mark you made with them, and how love is the only path you need to follow.

What to Do: Spend time today with someone you love dearly. Know that the love you share is a lasting legacy that will never perish.

Footsteps

A message about walking between worlds.

Hearing footsteps in an empty room can be unsettling. The unmistakable sound of footsteps in a particular corner of your home or even during specific times of the day or night may be a sign from the departed. Making noise in the physical plane requires a large amount of energy from those who have crossed over. When you hear these sounds and are certain they are more than just a building's unique settling sounds, you can rest easy knowing that a soul is sending you a sign from the other side. Their steps are meant to comfort you, and the ability for them to create the sound to do so is due to a certain bond you share with them (perhaps they are a departed loved one, or the person who previously lived in your home). They are walking between worlds, and one day you will walk there too.

What to Do: Take note of the time(s) and location(s) you hear the footsteps. Reflect on the person who you intuitively feel is sending you this sign, and send back a feeling of validation and gratitude as you do so.

Forget-Me-Not

An affirmation of eternal connection.

In grief, it can feel as though the bond you shared with the departed has been severed completely. The appearance of the forget-me-not flower, either in its physical form or in artistic depictions, assures you that this feeling is far from reality. The forget-me-not is a symbol of eternal connection in the spiritual realm. It is a communication from the other side that the bonds of love you share are incapable of being broken by death. This flower is often associated with keeping memories, love, and undying respect. When you see it, it's a message that your connection with the departed has endured and is still as strong as ever.

What to Do: Take time to remember the love you share in this world and beyond. Sit in the emotions of this strong affection and know that any feelings that arise aren't yours alone. They come from a spiritual source as well—a source that is sharing them with you now.

Communicating Back: Donate

Remembering those who have crossed over with an act of service or a monetary donation is a simple way to open up the channels of communication between yourself and the other side. Think about a space in which you can pay the energy forward as you honor their memory. Considering their own passions in this life, you can choose an organization or a cause to donate to in their honor. Volunteering at the animal shelter that they themselves would visit, giving a monetary gift to the place of worship they belonged to, and organizing a fundraiser for a cause they were invested in are all ways to create this conversation. The act of donating something creates a space of remembrance where those who've passed can connect, so you can enjoy their presence, memory, and messages.

Fox

A symbol sent to encourage your psychic wisdom.

The elusive fox glides through the forest confidently using its natural intelligence and intuition to guide it. Its adaptability and cleverness inspire respect and awe. The fox is often associated with ingenuity, protection, and observation. When you see this symbol, it is a strong encouragement from other side energy to trust your own inner intuition. You have the psychic ability to listen to what is happening in the non-physical realms, and that ability will be a faithful compass in guiding you through life's challenges and uncertainties. Observing your world with all of your senses, including your extrasensory ones like intuition, will be useful in the days to come.

What to Do: It's time to tap into your own psychic awareness! Start a meditation practice, work on opening your third eye, or pick up a book about spiritual intuition. Honing your psychic skills in daily life will allow you to open up to seeing more than others do.

Gemstone/Crystal

A spiritual acknowledgment of how special you are.

When you feel suddenly attracted to a gemstone or crystal, pay close attention. There may be more to it than just finding it pretty. Gemstones and crystals are often infused with meanings, which is why humans have long attributed them to special strengths, powers, and spiritual insights. Repeatedly noticing certain stones or finding yourself curious about a stone's particular properties may be a result of a spiritual energy sending you a message from the other side. Receiving the sign of amethyst, for example, signifies a need for calm in your life, while citrine encourages you to remain optimistic. Gemstones for your birthday, or the birthday of the one who crossed over, also have special significance, as they are more specifically tailored to you.

What to Do: When you feel connected to a certain stone, do research into its specific meaning, then find a way to wear it or carry it with you often.

Birth Month Symbols

The symbols universally associated with birth months are a go-to sign the departed enjoy sending. It is very possible that those frequent images of forget-me-nots or sapphires are cluing you in to a soul with a September birthday who is making contact. The bond of the birth month to the departed makes it a powerful touchstone for connection.

Geranium

A promise of protection and encouragement to heal.

Letting others in after experiencing loss can be a frightening thought. The geranium is a floral symbol that encourages healing while also assuring you that you're watched over and protected. When seeing this flower with consistency, either in its physical form or in artistic depictions, know that you are being comforted by a soul on the other side. They acknowledge the loss you've endured and fortify your ability to find connection again. Letting others in isn't taking away from the bond you had once shared with the departed; rather, it allows you to remember how to truly live again despite their physical absence.

What to Do: When feeling nudged by the appearance of a germanium symbol, think about someone you can let in who you've been holding at a distance. Having coffee with a new friend, joining a book club, or simply returning some phone calls to people who care about you can connect you to the space in you that is ready to continue your healing journey.

Grasshopper

A symbolic nudge to take advantage of opportunities now.

With its strong back legs allowing it to leap freely, navigate diverse landscapes, and swiftly escape danger, the grasshopper has been a longstanding symbol throughout time. It's often associated with prosperity, good luck, and the ability to transform. The grasshopper symbol emphasizes your own ability to move when necessary, reminding you that you are always able to make a change when the situation calls for it. Seeing a grasshopper is a message of motivation from those who have crossed over. You are being encouraged to take on new opportunities coming your way. You might have many fears when doing so, but this symbol assures you that your adaptability and positive energy will successfully see you through.

What to Do: Reflect on a few opportunities that have come your way of late. New beginnings are sometimes disguised as changes you don't feel up for. Have you recently declined a promotion or brushed off a meetup with a new set of friends? Perhaps it's time to reconsider an option you previously shrugged off.

Handprint

A strong sign of the link between you and another.

Left behind as a mark of what once was, a handprint is a reminder that while a person's time here on Earth is temporary, their impact lasts forever. Handprints are often very personal symbols for one's spiritual identity, connection, and belonging. When you are seeing handprints repeatedly, know that a soul is letting you know that the connection you share hasn't dissolved. Handprints have often been seen as spiritual gateways, suggesting that the separation between this world and the next is simply an illusion. When you see this symbol, the departed is telling you that they are with you in many ways, even though they are no longer in their physical form. Much like hands touching palm to palm, divided by a pane of glass, a spiritual energy is making their presence known to you now.

What to Do: Outline your own handprint and hang it somewhere you can see it often. Think about the connection you and those who have crossed over share and how it still lives on today.

Communicating Back:
Repurpose Their Belongings

When you need to organize and pack up the belongings of a person who has crossed over, the feeling of overwhelm can be almost unmanageable. The things that a soul leaves behind in this material world were important to them and carry energy that can be strongly felt (especially when you have to take care of removing them). Thoughtfully repurposing belongings can be a helpful way to connect with the departed as you take on this difficult task. Those on the other side enjoy their material possessions in a new way when they cross over: When put to good use, these items and their value become a significant spiritual connection. Sending cherished books to a community library, good-quality suits to an organization that gives them to those in need, or heirloom collectables to a local museum to put on display is a way you can keep the energy of those on the other side close by.

Hawk

Advice to strengthen your spiritual gifts.

Given the magnificence of this bird when it soars in the sky, it's no wonder the hawk is highly regarded as a messenger of the gods. Its keen ability to see from afar is a reminder to look at the whole picture before making a move. It is often associated with protection, guardianship, and spiritual awareness. The abilities you have to connect with the other side are being highlighted when seeing this bird in your life, and it signals you to take a new perspective to amplify these messages. Those who have crossed over are communicating with you, and to hear them, you'll need to become a spiritual conduit of your own making.

What to Do: Think about a few ways you can connect with your spiritual gifts and strengthen them. Take a meditation class, join up with a drum circle, or read a few books that fire up your spiritual curiosity!

Hawthorn (Leaf/Tree)

A symbol of healing hearts.

Laden with beautiful white flowers and thick, sharp thorns, the hawthorn tree holds deep spiritual significance for many. It has been renowned for its medicinal properties throughout the ages and is seen as a representation of wisdom and renewed life. The hawthorn tree symbolizes the purity of the soul that comes after adversity and grief. It blooms in spring, a reminder of the cycle of life. The appearance of this symbol in your life is a message of healing from the other side. Spiritual energy is validating that you have been through incredible suffering and the time for healing has finally arrived.

What to Do: Sit in the peace that you are ready to heal from the trials of the past. Know that you are on this healing journey with supportive energy by your side.

Heart (Shape)

A symbol of spiritual unity with a departed loved one.

When facing a life without the physical presence of someone dear to you, it can feel isolating and lonesome. Seeing the heart shape is a message from your loved one to you saying, "I am with you, always." The heart is a symbol of spiritual unity, connection, and the power of love to cross all barriers—even through death. This sign is coming to you because the one you miss wants you to know there is no force that could separate what really matters. The love you share is eternal and links you on a deep and fundamental level. You are never alone when you see this sign; your loved one is near you at this very moment.

What to Do: Draw this symbol often and find a way to incorporate it in your decor, even in small ways. Placing a heart-shaped trinket, paper doodle, or craft in a location where you can see it frequently will remind you that loving energy from the other side is with you when you focus on the eternal bond you share.

Seeing Shapes in Nature

Seeing shapes in nature can be a spiritual experience. Sticks lined up like 111, a circle of leaves made into a natural wreath, and a watermark that resembles a star are all ways a soul can make itself known. Seeing a certain shape regularly in nature and in varied ways is an even "louder" spiritual sign. For example, starting your morning seeing birds sitting in the shape of a heart, finding a heart-shaped stone in your path, and later looking up in the sky to see a cloud that is heart-shaped are all big alerts from a soulful presence. Seeing these shapes is a fun surprise—and an invitation to communicate right back with the one who is sending them! Arrange your own shapes in nature when possible and see how much stronger these signs become after you do so.

Heron

A symbolic validation of your fortitude.

The heron has mesmerized humans for years as it gracefully stands in ponds and wetlands with stoic stillness. This bird is revered for its mindfulness and beauty and is often associated with fortitude, wisdom, and patience. When you see this symbol, know that a soul on the other side is applauding your own inner strength. You've overcome many challenges in your life; you've built a foundation that cannot be disturbed even in the harshest conditions. The messenger of this sign sees that your character has grown even in great adversity and that your inner self carries a knowledge that was hard won.

What to Do: Think about what past trials and tribulations have taught you about the meaning of life and your purpose within it. Reflect on what you've learned and how you can prioritize these truths over things that are simply not important enough for your concern.

High Whistle/Ringing

An auditory sign that a supportive presence is with you.

Hearing the high whistle of wind skirting past, a pitched ring in your ear, or a melodious tune from seemingly nowhere may be a message from the departed alerting you to their supportive presence. Those who have crossed over can manipulate sound frequencies into high whistles, ringing, or eerie tunes to show you they are near. A soul is letting you know that they still care for you. They want you to continue your clairaudience, or clear hearing, strengthening it to receive more messages in this way.

What to Do: When you hear this noise, take a moment to center yourself and allow your senses to heighten. Lean into the noise and attempt to hear beyond the physical realm. The emotions, visions, and thoughts that come next are important, so take note of them!

HZ Frequencies

Hertz frequencies, or Hz frequencies, are thought to provide healing and balance for our mental and physical selves. They are also thought to pave an easier path for spiritual energies to enter the material realm so people can receive impactful messages. Playing them around your home or in your car or office is a soothing way to match your frequency to the spiritual energies that wish to communicate. Specifically, playing the 1074 Hz frequency (called the "spiritual frequency") can support spiritual correspondence and growth.

Holly

A cheerful promise of everlasting life.

Its striking deep green leaves against bright red berries sets the holly plant apart. Used for centuries for celebratory purposes, the holly holds deep symbolic meaning for many. Holly signifies protection, everlasting life, and prosperity. When you see this sign, know that a soul who has crossed over is sending you a cheerful promise of everlasting life. They have made the journey to the other side and are comforting you with this message. This sign is a celebration of the renewal that comes when life on this physical plane ends.

What to Do: Decorate and celebrate with the holly plant in any way that makes you feel joy. Place sprigs of it around your home, plant some in the garden, or craft with its image in some way. Be creative and feel spiritual energy celebrate with you.

Hummingbird

A spiritual signal to live life to the fullest.

This delicate bird is capable of amazing feats. It is the only bird that can fly backward, and it is an incredibly tenacious creature for its size. The hummingbird is a sign of joy, adaptability, and courage. When you see this symbol, spiritual energy on the other side is asking you to savor the moment. You are being encouraged to have fun, rest a little, and feel present in your joy. You have shown you are incredible and capable of many things.

What to Do: Think about how to live life to the fullest today. Have dessert before dinner, plan a trip you've been dreaming about, or take yourself out for a movie date. You deserve to have some fun in life.

Collections

Looking around your home you may notice you already have an affinity for a certain type of collectible. Perhaps you have an array of bear tchotchkes or you happen to have a real love for hummingbird wall art. Taking a closer look at what you find yourself collecting and why may give you some more clues to where this affection stems from. Additionally, calling in the energy of these symbols or beginning a collection that signifies a bond with a soul who has crossed over amplifies the connection.

Ibis

An encouraging symbol of guidance and higher purpose.

The ibis has an ability to observe its world with a keen eye. This bird is an ancient symbol of divine guidance, spiritual communication, and higher purpose. After suffering loss, trials, and tribulations, it can be difficult to know where to go next. The goals, motivations, and priorities you once felt so sure about can shift and become distorted in this new reality. Seeing the ibis is a message from those on the other side that you are being guided to a higher calling. Change is inevitable, and following your intuition is the path to your new world. You are being comforted and also encouraged to rebuild a life that aligns with what makes you feel purposeful.

What to Do: Think about what changes have happened since recent challenging times and consider where you can reprioritize some goals. New opportunities, relationships, and perspectives can be unfamiliar, but they are also a sign that you're ready to follow your new life purpose.

Adopting a Wild Animal

Feeling connected to a particular animal and seeing it repeatedly signifies that you are being sent a certain energy from the other side. One way you can further bring this energy into your life is through donating to this animal's protection in some way. An action such as symbolically adopting a wild animal from a reputable organization can send a bit of that energy back into the world. This type of gesture strengthens the meaning of this sign and helps you to fully embrace it. A gift of money in this way gives back not only to the animal itself, but also confirms to the one on the other side that you've indeed received their sign.

Ice Formation

A sign to be still and unlock your spiritual gifts.

The prisms of light refracted by an icicle hanging outside your window or the ice cubes in your glass catch the eye. They can give a sense of feeling frozen in time, a pure feeling of stillness. When you see this sign, the moment that comes with it is a message in and of itself. You are being reminded by someone on the other side to sit in silence—in your own personal stillness. This is where the connection to those who have passed on is forever alive, and this is where you are told to meet them at any time you feel the need. Ice represents purity, the illusion of time, and self-exploration. You are being guided to go within to unlock the spiritual gifts necessary to connect with the other side.

What to Do: Sit in stillness for a few minutes today and each day that follows. See how the silence of mind opens up the thoughts, feelings, and insights that have been locked within for a long time.

Impatiens

A message of adaptability and endurance.

The impatiens flower is a resilient one. It is uniquely able to thrive in shadows while needing very little maintenance to produce its beautiful blooms. Seeing this flower is a message from someone on the other side that you too are adaptable and able to endure much adversity. While you may feel weathered and diminished by the darkness you've suffered in life, the growth you've experienced has been there the whole time! You are being reminded that the difficulties you have suffered haven't dimmed your light, but rather brightened it as an inspiration for those who know you. The impatiens is also indicative of vitality and individuality. A soul's energy is letting you know they see your beauty and are proud of you.

What to Do: Take time today to reflect on how you have survived a trying time. Feel proud of yourself for making it through and living life each day while dealing with the loss you've endured.

Iris

A floral message to have faith in the signs you see.

There is so much that people don't know about where the departed venture when they cross over. The iris flower symbolizes faith, divine protection, and wisdom. It has long been associated with the promise of good news and of communication between worlds. Those who cross over send this symbol to call your attention to their new ways of contacting you. When you see this flower often, either in its physical form or in artistic depictions, know that the departed wants you to have faith in the signs you see. They're saying to you, "I am sending you something good."

What to Do: When confronted with this symbol repeatedly, sit in solitude for a few moments and repeat, "I open myself up to your messages." Afterward, you may find yourself noticing a lot more than you have in the past, and you'll be able to make the connections to those on the other side.

Communicating Back: Clean a Gravestone

The markers of a life once lived can be left to the forces of nature—especially once their own loved ones have joined them in the afterlife. Taking the time to clean up gravestones and the area surrounding them can connect you with other side energy. It's important to do this in a respectful manner so you don't disrupt the sanctity of the space. Having the intention of preserving a soul's memory in a spot that was meant to memorialize them directly touches upon the bond between realms, even if one between you never existed on this plane before. You may find yourself curious about their personal history and surviving family, and experience other inspired thoughts before, during, and after cleaning a gravestone. These are almost always spiritual communications from the soul you are assisting. Updating any surviving database that exists is also a lovely way to relay your own soulful message. Uploading a photo of the headstone to a dedicated website or alerting any caretakers of the property it lies upon allows their memory to endure for years to come.

Key

A symbol of your infinite potential.

Finding a key randomly in drawers, in the corner of your closet, or in your direct pathway is a powerful spiritual symbol. You are being asked to unlock your infinite potential. If you notice that your own keys are going missing and reappearing often, it's possible a soul on the other side is alerting you to the need to focus on a specific life purpose. As a sign, the key can refer to a new beginning, a hidden talent lying dormant, or even a solution to a present problem. The key is universally symbolic of knowledge, power, and the journey of the soul. Having interactions with keys in your physical reality or noticing their images following you in various forms means you're getting a spiritual nudge to do some inner work.

What to Do: Wear a key around your neck or decorate one on your keychain as a constant reminder of the faith someone on the other side has in you as you work to unlock the talents, purpose, and wisdom you contain.

Knocking

A sign of opportunities to come.

Hearing knocking on the door only to answer it and see no one there can set off your internal alarms. But although it's normal to react to this phenomenon with fear, the spiritual significance is quite positive. Knocks are auditory signs from those on the other side alerting you to change. There is energy in other realms that is actively working to open doors for you to new opportunities that will serve you well. Change is frightening, but chances are this is something you have been wanting for a long time and have been too afraid to initiate on your own. Spiritual energy is working to do this for you, and all you have to do is walk the path that will soon be cleared. This is a message to make way for positive change.

What to Do: Take note of the number of knocks you are hearing if they are occurring in sequences, as they can be pointing to specific tasks you need to complete right now to prepare for a coming change. Three knocks alert you to balancing your life; four knocks mean to focus on consistency; and five knocks are a clear signal that changes are imminent.

Ladybug

A symbolic recognition of a life-changing experience.

The small but colorful ladybug can nurture your own sense of inner peace with its gentle nature. The ladybug brings a sense of joy and hope for new beginnings. Symbolizing prosperity, transformation, and spiritual awakenings, this tiny creature packs a powerful metaphorical punch! It teaches that in the most unlikely moments, your life can irreversibly shift. When you see this symbol, a soul on the other side is recognizing a life-changing experience you're about to undergo. No matter how inconsequential it can seem in the moment, it is indeed a transformative one.

What to Do: Reflect on all the things that had to go right to bring you to this moment in the here and now. Send out some love and gratitude for the ones looking out for you on the other side; they will be with you through the changes ahead, in the heart space you have made for them.

License Plate

An assertive way to call your attention.

Recognizing initials, birth dates, or names spelled out on a license plate can surprise even the most skeptical. In this on-the-go world, license plates have become an easier way for those on the other side to grab your attention and assertively give a message. Seeing a plate from the state or province that the departed lived in, vanity plates that spell out their nickname, or even a number that resonates in some personal way, can be a sign from those on the other side. When you see this sign, you'll immediately feel as if they are speaking to you right in the moment.

What to Do: Have fun with this spiritual energy and ask those on the other side to show you some more signs on the road. On your next long drive, simply ask them to send you some signs that are unmistakably from them. Be patient when you do this and give gratitude by believing it when you see it!

Lilac

A loving message to open your heart.

The early bloom of the lilac is often the first to greet people in springtime. Its light scent is instantly recognizable and can invoke a sense of comfort and nostalgia for the past. The lilac has long been a symbol of the passing of time, joy, and memories of love. When noticing the recurring symbol of the lilac in your life, either in its physical form or in artistic depictions, a soul on the other side is saying, "Open your heart." They want you to know that there is a renewal happening in your life. Yet, no matter what life brings you next, the memories of your bond will always live in your heart.

What to Do: Take this time to sit and reflect on days gone by. Embrace the emotions that arise; letting these emotions in requires you to open your heart. Think about a time you felt loved by the one who crossed over.

Creative Symbols

As mentioned in Part 1 of this book, a sign isn't always a literal object. Those on the other side get creative with their delivery, and opening up your mind to noticing this allows for more connection. You may see symbols in their physical form, but you may also see artistic depictions and various other manifestations. For instance, seeing lilacs in a garden is one thing, but then being bombarded with their scent, photos and/or artwork of them, and storefront names with the word "lilac" in them can really solidify the sign. You may see someone in line in front of you with a lilac tattoo, notice that a screen name of a new friend incorporates the word "lilac," and later on receive a gift of a lilac candle. The possibilities for sending these types of messages are endless, which means when you open your mind, the ways in which the departed can now send them are limitless.

Lily

Acknowledgment that a soul has crossed over.

When someone leaves the physical world, you can still find yourself worrying about them. But rest assured: The lily flower is a symbolic message from a soulful energy that they have crossed over and are now reborn into their eternal life. The lily is often associated with purity, innocence, and eternal love. The lingering concern you may have for the departed can be comforted by the appearance of this flower in your daily life— either in its physical form or in artistic depictions. Note the colors of the lilies that you are seeing as well. Yellow brings with it a message of new beginnings and white brings one of rebirth, while pink and red suggest love, passion, and sweetness.

What to Do: When seeing the lily flower, envision a beautiful white light. Visualize those who have crossed over as happy and forever safe on the other side. Trust in the promise that one day you will be with them again.

Lion

A symbolic restoration of your inner power.

The iconic figure of the lion looming over the vast landscapes that it freely roams inspires power, strength, and ferocity. The lion is often a symbol for protection, nobility, and the strength within. This symbol entering your life is a message encouraging you to restore your inner power. The potential within you is abundant, and tapping into that potential is something those on the other side know you can do. Challenges and opposition in life can be faced with the strengthening of your own fortitude.

What to Do: Think about ways you can connect to your power today by getting out of your comfort zone. Complete a challenging workout, teach yourself a new skill, or cross off something on your bucket list. You are stronger than you know, and those on the other side are reminding you of your power.

Lizard

A spiritual reminder that change is positive.

The adaptable and mysterious behavior of the lizard has made it a foundational symbol in various cultures and belief systems. The lizard excels in diverse habitats and in some cases can regenerate its tail and skin when damaged. Because of this, it generally represents survival, rebirth, and resilience. It is also often seen as an esteemed spiritual guide that offers pathways to illumination and enlightenment. When you see this symbol, know that you are being reminded that change is positive. You can thrive in new environments because you are more resilient than you may realize. There is a transformation within that will come when you change the environment around you, and it's a positive one.

What to Do: Reflect on which changes in life you've been fighting against. Think about where you can shift your energy toward adaptability rather than controlling an inevitable outcome. Spiritual energy is reaffirming that you will be renewed when your environment changes.

Lotus

A symbol of fortitude and perseverance.

The lotus flower grows in adverse conditions, blooming beautifully in places other flowers can't. When you see this flower, know that a soulful energy is validating that you have overcome extreme adversity. You may have felt alone in your struggles, but the departed are making their presence known to you now. The lotus flower is symbolically used to connect with negative emotions to aid you in accepting them and allowing something beautiful to grow from them. In either its physical form or in artistic depictions entering your life, this symbol of fortitude and perseverance is a strong validation of your strength.

What to Do: Sit quietly and picture your recent struggles. Feel your perspective shift as you give yourself gratitude and praise for a job well done under the difficult circumstances.

Magnolia (Leaf/Flower/Tree)

A loving sign of everlasting bonds.

The magnolia tree is able to endure the harshest conditions, blooming despite the endless hardships it faces in the natural world. It symbolizes longevity, courage, and endurance, and it is a sign of everlasting connection. When you receive this sign, know that a spiritual energy is affirming that the connection you have is eternal. The separation between you and the departed is a challenge you both have faced and survived, each in your own way. This symbol reassures you that what is between you can never fade; it can only grow stronger and bloom with continued remembrance.

What to Do: Use the magnolia in some way. Place a bouquet of the flowers on your table, plant a tree in your garden, or incorporate the flower or leaf print in your wardrobe. In doing so, know that you are keeping the connection between you and the departed strong.

Mail

A profound delivery from the other side.

Receiving a seemingly misdirected letter or package with the departed's initials or name on it may be more than just a clerical error at the post office! Those on the other side will often send mail your way that has been altered to show you they were behind this postal mishap. You may find yourself in possession of your neighbors' package but with your late mother's name on it, or a piece of mail that was meant for them but made its way to you instead. A soul is sending you a profound delivery with this sign, one that lets you know they are still present.

What to Do: If possible, keep the memento of this afterlife delivery in a place where you can remind yourself they are still nearby. If you must return the package, write out your emotions in this moment and the gratitude you want to send to the departed.

Communicating Back: Write a Letter

Just because someone has crossed over doesn't mean you can't still drop them a line, send a text, or write a letter! In fact, doing so calls their energy closer to you. When you speak to them as if they are still alive, they can act stronger in spirit moving forward. Picking up your phone and "calling" them, commenting on their memorialized social media page, or writing them a letter in your journal still delivers your message, albeit in a different way than if they were in the physical world.

Maple (Leaf/Tree)

Otherworldly encouragement to center yourself.

The sturdy maple tree withstands harsh conditions by being adaptable, resilient, and firm in its strong roots. This tree symbolizes perseverance, the importance of foundation, and transformation. Shedding its leaves for the winter to come is a reminder that you too must let go in order to survive. Its root system anchors it firmly to the ground, reminding you to take care of your own fundamental beliefs and foundations. Seeing this symbol is an otherworldly message to let go of what no longer serves you and center yourself on who you are within. There is someone on the other side asking you to remember where you came from and revive the foundational beliefs, lessons, and heart connections that contributed to who you are today.

What to Do: Revisit old photographs in order to jog your memory of the lessons of your early years. Stay focused on how you've grown strong because of the adversity you've weathered and recenter yourself around this wisdom.

Marigold

A strong symbol of interworld togetherness.

Grieving the loss of those who have crossed into the next realm is part of how they stay in your memory. The darkness of forgetting them is a fear that no one wants realized. The brilliant colors of the marigold flower are reminiscent of the sun's guiding light and warmth, representing the shining of a light upon the memory of who you lost. This flower is associated with honoring those who have left this world as well as paving the way to the unseen realms where the departed now dwell. Seeing this flower either in its physical form or in artistic depictions is a message from those who have passed over that there is connection between worlds. This is a reminder that life and death are intertwined, and the veil between the physical and spiritual realms is thinner than you may realize.

What to Do: Honor the departed in some way today. Tell a story about them, place a favorite photo of them in your home, or wear something that reminds you of them. Remembering your unique connection binds you to them forever!

Money

A sign of concern, care, and abundance from the other side.

Unexpected money showing up in your life is more than just a lucky occurrence! Those who have crossed over show you their care and concern by sending money in synchronistic ways. It becomes a metaphor for abundance, prosperity, and consideration. Receiving funds that seem happenstance, yet tie into a particular life event in a way that feels more than coincidental, is the departed's personal sign to you. Seeing money lying next to a grave you're visiting, being gifted an amount that correlates to a loved one's birthday, and even receiving an inheritance you weren't expecting are all ways in which a soul is letting you know that they send you continued prosperity in this world from the next.

What to Do: Paying it forward in even the smallest way can reciprocate your gratitude back to whoever sent this sign. Buy someone a coffee, send a card to a mutual friend, or simply leave some change out at a register for the next person who needs it.

Moth

A message of comfort as a chapter ends.

The moth is associated with endings, shadow work, and transition. It's often linked with the negative and darker aspects of life and its cycles. However, its ability to transform through metamorphosis gives hope to new beginnings. The darkness you sometimes walk through sheds old beliefs, and just like the moth turning from a caterpillar into its winged adult form, you are reborn. The moth is a spiritual message of comfort as well as an acknowledgment of the trials and suffering you've undergone.

What to Do: Shadow work is the exploration of uncomfortable emotions. Take some time today to sit in the complicated feelings you've been having lately. Talk about them with a friend or a therapist or journal about what it is you feel the need to say.

Communicating Back: Plan a "Celebration of Life" Party

The energy of those on the other side can grow through laughter and happiness directed toward their memory. Creating joy by planning a "Celebration of Life" party to honor them is a way to enhance the vibration of your connection. Play music they enjoyed, serve their favorite foods, and share some fun memories in their honor. Ask guests to bring a photo to display and have them write down a memory, joke, or personal story that involves the departed. Afterward, collect all the tributes and place them in a special box or album to further this joyous bond.

Nail/Screw/Bolt

A spiritual symbol of stability.

Finding random nails, screws, or bolts throughout your day can be considered a pretty universal occurrence, but the meaning shifts when you look at it through a symbolic lens. Nails, screws, and bolts have a spiritual significance of stability, strength, and the capability to overcome. When you spot these items in your path and have no idea where they came from, know that a soul on the other side is encouraging you to put down roots, hold on to what you find important, and invest your time and energy. This could be a relationship worth pursuing, a financial investment, or a continued educational path. There is a need for you to remain steadfast in who you are and what you prioritize because this is the foundation for your future. You are being told to set your goals and stick to them moving forward.

What to Do: Reflect on what you have been feeling most passionate about lately. It could be an area of study you wish to pursue or a commitment to a wellness routine. Consider where you can take action and give more of yourself to this area of your life.

New Relationship

An extension of love from the other side.

After the death of a loved one, a void is created that is never truly filled. However, meeting someone who contributes to the role of the departed can not only help in healing and moving forward from that loss, but can also be a way that those on the other side send you their love. A new friend, love interest, or person who reminds you of the type of relationship that was lost is your loved one's way of making sure you still feel supported and seen. You may also receive this sign from those you didn't know personally but who are invested in a mutual mindset, like a coworker who helps you get a job done.

What to Do: Notice the new relationships that have made their way into your life lately. Consider how someone on the other side could be behind this meetup.

Fortuitous Connections

Those on the other side often have an invested interest in making sure you meet the right people so that their work isn't left unfinished. Meeting a new romantic partner not long after the passing of your very protective father can be a way that he is making sure you are safe. Finding the right partner that will ensure the legacy of a business is protected may be the work of the departed previous owner.

Oak (Leaf/Tree)

A sturdy sign of encouragement and strength.

The oak tree, with its deep roots and broad branches, provides stability in an often unstable natural world. This tree represents security, protection, and inner strength. When seeing this tree (or its leaves) often, you are being sent a boon of spiritual support. You are receiving an acknowledgment of your own ability to endure, ground yourself, and provide stability for yourself and others. Notice how this sign takes its place in your life in all forms, from leaves in your path to artistic depictions that grab your attention. There is a team of soulful energy around you making sure you aren't alone in your endeavors.

What to Do: Think about ways you can accomplish a current goal through your own determination and grit.

Object Moving

An unmistakable sign of a soul's proximity.

A window suddenly closing or a vase moving across a table on its own can certainly send a chill down your spine, but it can also be a good sign! When you see objects moving on their own, without any logical environmental cause, it is often an unmistakable sign that a departed soul is nearby. The energy it takes in order for those on the other side to make themselves known in this way is tremendous and requires a strong connection. Therefore, when you see this happening, take comfort in the fact that the energy you share with this spirit is unified, strong, and reciprocated across realms. This is proof that you are seeing signs regularly and giving gratitude to the one you know is sending them. Moving objects is the departed's way of saying, "Thank you, and I am here with you now."

What to Do: Give a word of thanks out loud to the one you know is sending you this colossal sign. Make sure to tell others who you know will appreciate this news as well, so this sign can touch their lives the way it has touched yours.

Orb

A photo-based sign with personal meaning.

The fuzzy orbital blur on your photo could be dust or a seemingly explainable camera anomaly. But it also could be a signal from someone on the other side who wants you to know that they are nearby. The spiritual presence of those who have crossed over is often associated with the transparent bubbles of light that can appear in photos. Those on the other side no longer have a physical body, but they can manifest their spiritual energy in this way. In fact, it's very common for those who have passed to play with the technology in images to get your attention. And while it's easier to catch these signs with the use of photography, you may also see orbs with the naked eye, as circular balls of visible light that seem to float with purpose.

What to Do: Take multiple photos when around family, friends, or even in spaces where you feel spiritual energy. Compare them and notice when and how you see orbs appear. You may notice a specific pattern that can't be explained by mere logic.

Orb Colors

Orbs are a language of their own design. Depending on who is sending them and what their purpose is, you will find countless interpretations when you look closer at this sign. One important thing to note is the color of the orbs you see, as each color holds a specific spiritual message:

- **White:** The soul of the loved one is with you.

- **Blue:** Your loved one wants you to know they are healed and at peace.

- **Green:** You are being sent joy and gratitude from the other side.

- **Gold:** You are being reminded that the soul is eternal and love never dies.

Owl

Spiritual acknowledgment that you see what others do not.

With its wide eyes and ability to navigate the darkness, the owl has long been thought to see worlds that others do not. This bird is a symbol with many meanings, but perhaps the most consistent of them all is the ability to see beyond. It is also associated with decision-making, great change, and wisdom through hard times. When you are noticing the owl in your life, a spiritual source is sending you a message that you also can see past the physical realm. Through the intuition of your heart, you have an unlimited ability to connect, see, and perceive the spiritual world and the signs it sends your way.

What to Do: Notice how you feel when you see the symbol of the owl. The feelings and emotions that surround this symbol are directly connected to its meaning and what the intended message is. What you are meant to see, you will first see in your heart.

Pain

A physical manifestation of a soul's message.

Feeling pain radiating from a spot where you know a departed soul had suffered an affliction in life has significance. Spirits will use clairsentience, or clear feeling, to send messages through physical pain sensors. Noticing that your chest feels heavy after the passing of a loved one due to a heart condition and feeling nerve pain radiating up your leg when thinking of someone who suffered a circulatory condition are ways that those on the other side can create a meaningful connection to you. You may notice the pain feeling like a shadow pain, or a lesser pain than what you would expect it to be. You may also find that you have this sensation when you're around people who lost someone you didn't personally know, but who is trying to send a message through you. If you are generally sensitive to energy, this is a way the departed will give proof of their enduring presence.

What to Do: When feeling this type of pain, take a moment to consider what its message might be. For example, experiencing a fleeting migraine when looking at a picture of someone who passed from an aneurysm could be a strong call of attention from the departed. When acknowledged, this type of pain will disappear immediately. If any pain persists, you should consider consulting a professional.

Palm (Leaf/Tree)

A signal of triumph, vitality, and peace.

The palm tree is naturally flexible, and this flexibility can also be seen in the various symbolic meanings it holds for many cultures and religions. Due to its long lifespan, it's a symbol for eternal life, and because it bears fruit, it also represents fertility and abundance. The palm tree universally symbolizes triumph over challenges, the vitality of one's spirit, and the peace that is well deserved after hard work. The palm leaf represents value and respect. When you see a palm leaf or tree symbol, know that a heavenly energy is signaling that you've deserved your rest after a tireless endeavor.

What to Do: Think about the amazing feats you've accomplished recently. Feel the pride and satisfaction someone on the other side is showing for you.

Communicating Back: Connect with a Tree

When receiving tree symbols and feeling pulled to particular types of trees, connecting spiritually can bring their powerful energy closer to you. Try sitting next to a tree you feel an affinity toward. Then, draw the energy of the tree into your thoughts and take note of visuals, inspired ideas, or emotions that come forward when you do so. You may also want to collect ethically sourced objects made from the wood of that type of tree, as these are powerful touchstones for manifesting spiritual messages!

Panther

A mystical sign of protection and knowledge.

The panther slinks through its habitat, patiently waiting to make its next move. Its black fur and fierce form have captivated people across cultures and civilizations. It represents many ideals, including transformation, power, and ferocity. Seeing this symbol is a sign from the other side that you are protected in your quest for knowledge and inner wisdom. The new curiosities you have and interests you are forming are important catalysts of transformation. You are being guided to practice some introspection and encouraged to embrace the necessary changes that are coming.

What to Do: Dive headfirst into an interest you've been on the fence about. Take actions today to get started on something that makes you feel interested and curious. Be mindful of what new spiritual insights come your way as a result of this pursuit.

Peacock

A reminder that the soul is eternal.

Everyone admires the peacock for its breathtaking feathers. It has long been a symbol of power, beauty, and the cosmic connection to human life. The peacock's feathers shed and regrow annually, which is why this bird is often associated with immortality, transcendence, and rebirth. It reminds you that you too have the ability to transcend and reawaken to a new life after this physical one has ended. When you see a peacock, it's a message from someone on the other side that the soul is eternal. Your life here is temporary, but eternal continuation awaits you on the other side.

What to Do: Explore your personal connection to spirituality and your soul growth through a daily journaling routine or by checking out books that ignite your soul's curiosity.

Perfume

A gentle signal of a soulful presence.

A waft of a familiar scent brings forth an immediate personal connection. Catching a signature smell that takes you back to your grandmother's vanity, your aunt's signature scent, or your late father's favorite cologne is a bittersweet experience. Perfumed scents appearing out of thin air, and disappearing just as swiftly, aren't just your mind playing tricks on you. The departed will use your clairalience, or clear smelling abilities, to grab your attention. And it isn't just those you've known who may drop these scented signals: Anyone on the other side wishing to connect may send you this sign, indicating their personalized greetings. When you smell something that reminds you of someone who has crossed over or simply captures your attention due to its unfamiliarity, know that a soul is present right now.

What to Do: Recreate a meaningful scent during a meditation or quiet moment. Know that as you do so, you are connecting with a spirit's personalized presence yet again.

Pet Behavior

Your pet's way of showing you the beyond.

As most pet owners know, patterned behaviors are a part of an animal's personality. However, when a pet's actions, vocalizations, and other habits have suddenly changed out of nowhere, and with no medical explanation, it could be a sign of a soul making contact. Animals are able to walk between worlds and feel energy far better than people can. Seeing a dog bark at a seemingly empty corner, noticing your cat batting at an unseen object, and even experiencing your pet repeating behaviors of a departed animal can all be signs from beyond. Pets can allow the energy of those who've crossed over to flow through them. They may begin acting in a way that reminds you of a loved one or a departed pet. You may also notice them interacting with what appears to be nothing, in an attempt to get you to notice what they see so clearly.

What to Do: Observe your pet's actions with a keen eye. Use your emotional intuition to consider other energies that may be present and impacting their strange actions.

Animal Visits

Animals are natural conduits for those on the other side. It's not uncommon for a stray cat to show up at your door immediately after the passing of a loved one, or to find yourself rescuing a dog soon after their death. It's also something that can occur when a soul you didn't know in life wants to make contact with you. Perhaps you notice a friendly bird constantly tapping on your window after moving into a new home or encounter a friendly squirrel when you are at work. It's possible those with connections to the buildings you are in or the work you do will send signs through animal visitations. The comfort and companionship an animal brings are just what a soul needs to attach to in order to make contact. By nurturing these new relationships with your animal visitors, you will feel more connected to the bond you and the departed share.

Phone Call

A symbolic connection to the other side.

A call from a departed person's phone number could easily be blamed on a crossing of wires in this glitchy tech world. However, the significance changes when you consider the fact that it's a common way for those on the other side to make contact. Receiving a call or a voicemail from the departed's phone number could be their way of letting you know they are all right on the other side. A call from an unknown number where you hear a faded or muted voice that sounds familiar to theirs, or even sounds like a recording they had on their own devices, is another way those who've crossed over will attempt to make their presence known. Energy on the other side can manipulate technology in the physical world to get their messages across!

What to Do: When receiving this sign, know that the primary purpose is to reassure you they are safe, secure, and at peace. Take a moment to appreciate that you were able to receive such a powerful correspondence.

Pinecone

A sign of inner awakening.

The pinecone is an ancient symbol that has been used to convey different meanings for thousands of years. Its circular shape holds hundreds of seeds and assists with the pine tree's regeneration. Because of this, it often symbolizes rebirth, renewal, and regeneration. The concentric shape holds deep meaning as well, as it is thought to mirror the pineal gland, or the gland responsible in humans for the perception of light. This gland is often referred to as your physical third eye; because of this, the pinecone symbolizes enlightenment and inner spiritual awakenings. When you encounter this symbol, know that you are receiving an otherworldly sign asking you to awaken your soul. You are being directed to further your own awareness of self and the spiritual world around you.

What to Do: Consider how you can increase your spiritual knowledge. Pick up a book that interests you and/or talk to like-minded friends about spiritual awakenings, and journal your experiences in the process.

Playing Card

A playful sign to raise your awareness.

A playing card seemingly discarded on the sidewalk or tucked into your windshield wiper can seem like littering to the untrained eye. But a playing card can actually be a playful way someone on the other side is trying to make you aware of the language of signs. Where you see this card (or multiple cards) and how it is placed—face up or down—and consistent suits or even significant variations of multiple cards can all tell their own unique tale. Perhaps the card numbers have personal significance, or a series of cards found over time become hands, such as flushes or a full house. All of these can hold layered meanings in your relationship with the departed. The cards could be physical in form, pop-ups on your laptop, or even artistic depictions. Chances are the one sending you these messages had a mischievous and spirited personality of their own in life. And now they're bringing you a puzzle to solve so you can play along with them!

What to Do: Either collect or take photos of the cards you are seeing. You'll begin to notice a pattern over time that can clue you in to an even larger and more personal message.

Items Falling

If you've been seeing fallen picture frames, experienced books dropping at your feet as you walk by, or spotted an item that belonged to the departed appearing askew, it could be a purposeful sign. In order to get your attention and let you know they are still present, those on the other side can move things with significance. A book that seems to have a strong personal meaning falling in your path, or a picture of your late grandfather toppled over, is a little way they let you know they didn't go anywhere at all. Reflect on what is repeatedly being moved or falling and what significance it has to those in spirit as well as yourself. When you place the items back where they belong, give a little gratitude for the energy that was spent in sending you this spiritual nudge. It takes a lot of effort for someone on the other side to manipulate the physical world!

Praying Mantis

A spiritual symbol of stillness.

The praying mantis's cunning ability to remain completely still, blending in with its surroundings, is what establishes it as a meaningful sign. It has long been thought to be a symbol of prayer, divine guidance, and inner stillness. In many cultures it also represents the connection to spiritual energy. Seeing this sign is a message that you are burdened by a worried and cluttered mindset. The struggles of daily life and the anxious thoughts that plague you are causing you to lose your attachment to the other side—an attachment that a spiritual source is asking you to notice again. This is a direct message suggesting stillness so that you may reestablish the ethereal ties between yourself and the spirit.

What to Do: Take five to ten minutes today to sit in a meditative state. Breath slowly and allow any cluttered thoughts and intrusive ideas to simply float away.

Presence

A signal that you're not alone.

Feeling like you're in the presence of someone, even when you are in fact totally alone, isn't always your imagination running wild. Feeling stared at, walked past, or as if there is a person sitting beside you is a strong sign that a soul is nearby. The loneliness that accompanies loss can be immense, and sensing a presence is a way that those who've crossed over can alleviate that feeling, both for themselves and you. There are many ways this sign from the departed can manifest. You may feel wary to sit on a certain chair as if you "feel" someone else occupying it. It's possible you sense a weight on a bed you are cuddled up in for the night, as if someone has just sat down on the edge of it. At times, you can feel as if someone has just run past you. In all these circumstances, your energy field is sensing what your physical eyes can't see. The sense of their presence is a soul's way of saying, "I am here with you; you are never alone."

What to Do: Consider who you feel is with you at this time. Perhaps you feel an added motivation to renovate your new home as the prior owner may have wanted, or simply sense the love of your uncle who has recently left this world. Investigate your emotions and observe them with an open and curious mind, as they will clue you in to the soul that is present with you.

Queen Anne's Lace

A floral representation of sanctuary, safety, and love.

When you look at the feathery leaves and delicate buds of the Queen Anne's lace flower, it's not hard to understand how it got its name. This lace-like flower has often been the symbol of home, sanctuary, and loving support. It is associated with protection and a feeling of delicacy. There are times in life when you might feel fragile, and Queen Ann's Lace is a message from the departed saying, "You are safe." Even when you feel unsure about navigating this wild world, a soulful energy is coming through with this symbol, encouraging you to feel their presence and create structure around the bond that will always exist between you.

What to Do: Think about a way you can make yourself feel more secure in your environment today. Create a cozy space in your home, make yourself a hearty meal, or treat yourself to a pleasant afternoon with a good book and a cup of tea.

Communicating Back: Plant a Nature Garden

Create a space where energies from this realm and the next can coexist by planting a memorial garden for the departed. It can be as large or small as your space and energy allow; however, make sure it's made with their memory in mind. Thinking about their preferences will help you plan the garden. You may add plants, flowers, or herbs you know they favored, or even a tree you associate with them. You could add an engraved plaque in their honor and/or imprint cement tiles with handprints, special messages, or stones. If this garden is in a public space, facilitating projects where members of the community can contribute is a lovely way of heightening the spiritual connection. Use the garden as a space to rest, meditate, and feel at peace. Visit the garden often, and take note of what special animals visit, as well as what nature signs and emotions arise. Consider it a space where nature signs hold space for communications from the other side.

Rabbit

A spiritual recommendation to alter your course.

The rabbit swiftly bounds across the landscape, its quick movements and fuzzy appearance capturing the attention of humans throughout time. Various meanings are associated with this animal across cultures. It is often seen as a symbol of abundance, sensitivity, and intuition. Some also connect the rabbit to the spiritual journeys people must take in life, as this animal is seen as the overseer of such quests. When you see a rabbit, you are receiving a recommendation to alter a current course you are on. The rabbit's ability to gracefully shift course, even while traveling at a high speed, is a suggestion for you to do the same.

What to Do: Think about a path of action you are currently taking that may not be the best choice for you. Perhaps a recent relationship has red flags that require your reflection, or you may need to alter your course of study if you are pursuing a degree. It's okay to say no or reconsider your options. Sit with your intuitive wisdom and find a path that works better for you!

Raccoon

A spiritual message of resourcefulness.

The sly raccoon has a reputation for playfulness and mischief. Thanks to behavior like getting into garbage cans and stealing pet food, along with its distinct face markings, the raccoon has been associated with being a trickster, along with self-reliance, intelligence, and creativity. When you see a raccoon, it's a message from the other side to tap into your own resourcefulness. You are more than capable of using the skills you already have in order to get through life's current challenges. A spiritual source is sending you guidance and encouragement in solving these problems.

What to Do: Reflect on a challenging situation that needs to be resolved. You may have hit a wall in receiving that career promotion, or realize that your current budget is never going to cover the dream vacation you have your heart set on. Consider how you can use what you already know to devise a new plan for tackling the challenge at hand. A new perspective, combined with your own resourcefulness, is all you need to solve the issue.

Rainbow

A colorful sign of hope and joy.

After losing someone special to you, the rainbow can become a sign of hope and connection. Just like the appearance of a rainbow after a storm, this symbol is there to remind you of the positive transformation and new beginnings that come from life's challenges. Rainbows that appear in nature or art, or even rainbow-themed gifts, can be taken as a sign that you are still connected to those you've lost. Double rainbows in nature accentuate the message of hope, joy, and your eternal bond.

What to Do: Fill yourself with the gratitude of this sign and think about how you can live life to the fullest today. Face a small fear, do a mini meditation, or play with your pets to seize the day.

Enthusiasm for a Community Project

Those on the other side often connect to people who are helpers, volunteers, and active members of local organizations they themselves had an investment in. The contagious enthusiasm of community helpers in spirit strengthens when they connect with similar energy. A curator of the local history museum who feels compelled to protect and ensure the legacy of this space for generations to come and the music teacher who is driven to repair students' instruments may be examples of this spiritual bond.

Raven

A spiritual suggestion that magic exists all around you.

The dark form of the raven has long symbolized mystical exploration, death as a rebirth, and magical wisdom. It is no wonder that many cultures revere its mysterious nature and attribute its presence as one of protection and realms unseen. When you see this symbol, know that a spiritual source is asking you to see the magic that exists in the world. Even though you may not be able to physically see the alternate planes of existence that souls travel, that doesn't mean you can't look for evidence of them in signs and connections that already exist in your life. New beginnings come when you are looking at things in a new way; a soulful energy wants you to notice the magic so they can send you more.

What to Do: Open yourself up to the magic you may have been dismissing or shrugging off. The perfect friend made at the right time, repeating numbers, and the bird visiting your windowsill can now all be looked at with fresh eyes. Wonder, joy, and meaning can be found in the smallest of signs. Believe in the possibility that there is more than just what you experience in this human form.

Repeated Number

A numeric sign pointing you in a specific direction.

Seeing a repeated number (or numbers) throughout your day on receipts, mailboxes, advertisements, etc., can begin to feel a bit more than coincidental. Noticing that your morning coffee adds up to $5.55, being directed to 555 Main Street for your doctor's appointment, and then later seeing a billboard of a relator with "55" or "555" in their phone number aren't just happenstance. Those who have crossed over will use repeated numbers as a way to point out their continued presence. They can also send their own birthdays, death dates, or other significant dates or number sequences repeatedly to gain your curiosity and attention. The energy on the other side is able to manipulate not only your attention, but the frequency at which numbers vibrate, allowing them to use this tool to send you a specific message.

What to Do: Keep a record of the repeating numbers you see to make sense of them in your personal life. Look deeper into their specific meanings within angel numbers and numerology, either online or in a reference book. Also note whoever is at the forefront of your mind when you see these signs: Chances are they are the one responsible for sending you this sign.

Communicating Back:
Use Numbers As a Touchstone

Using numbers that are significant to those who have passed is an immediate way to make spiritual contact. Adopting their birth date, an important anniversary, or even the jersey number they had in school into your daily life will instantly inspire their closeness to you. Creating usernames with the numbers, doodling them, or even incorporating them into a passcode you use often can alert the departed to your attention. You can plan an important event on a date reflective of the numbers, or use the numbers symbolically as a theme for favors, prizes, or gifts at a party. Numbers communicate high-vibrational frequencies that are easy for a soul to respond to. Drawing in their energy this way is a welcome invitation and just may empower them to send you more of their own signs as well!

Robin

A soul's reassurance that they are at peace.

After losing someone close to you, it can be difficult to imagine them in a space beyond the physical realm. However, seeing a robin after the death of a loved one can fill you with an undeniable sense of tranquility. The robin holds special meaning; as it returns in the springtime after a harsh winter, it symbolizes hope, renewal, and the soul's journey. Seeing a robin is a message from your loved one that their soul has crossed the threshold to the next world and that they are at peace. The robin is a joyful bird, carrying love between worlds.

What to Do: When you see a robin, allow your heart to be filled with peace and joy as your loved one intends. Know they are safe and well taken care of and they want you to feel the love they hold for you eternally in their hearts.

Rose

A floral affirmation of the miracle of love.

When you lose someone you deeply love, the grief and pain you experience can feel insurmountable. But the rose is a message from the departed that the love you share will never truly die, even if their physical form has left this realm. This flower is a symbolic reminder from that loved one, simply stating, "I love you." Note the colors of the rose(s) you are seeing, as they have more nuanced meanings. Red symbolizes passion, pink communicates gratitude, white represents the purity of the soul, and yellow denotes joy.

What to Do: Reflect on the miracles that are created by love shared between you and the one(s) you miss. Think about how the love you give others may have changed them as well.

Communicating Back: Use a Meaningful Scent

Those on the other side may use scents to alert you to their presence. You also use scents to draw them in. A perfume that a loved one adored, a fragrance that reminds you of the departed, and certain essential oils are all effective in communicating back to a spirit. Spray the departed's signature perfume while thinking of them, fill your space with the scent of the floral sign they have been sending you, or diffuse essential oils such as juniper or lavender to clear stuck energy in order to make a path for higher vibrations and spiritual connections.

Rowan (Leaf/Tree)

A vibrant symbol of the vitality of life.

Since ancient times, the rowan tree has been planted beside homes to ward off negative forces. This tree, with its cyclical changes throughout the seasons, represents the vitality of life, as well as courage and protection. It's often referred to as "The Tree of Life," as it is associated with themes of resilience and overcoming adversity. When seeing this symbol, you are being alerted to forces around you that require your own spiritual fortification in order to endure. You are being offered spiritual protection while you call forward your own vitality and resilience at this time.

What to Do: Reflect on where you are needing to build up your strengths in daily life. Perhaps you are being called to pay closer attention to your health and wellness, or being encouraged to confront those who wish to take advantage of you. Whatever it may be, know that you are not alone in your efforts.

Sacred Geometry

**An ancient symbol meant to strengthen
your spiritual foundation.**

The foundational shapes of the natural world hold great spiritual meaning. A spiral of a snail's shell and the hexagonal cell of a honeycomb are examples of sacred geometry in the everyday world. There are also complex forms of these shapes, such as the interlocking circles of the ancient "Seed of Life." Sacred geometry is a sign that you are ready to strengthen your spiritual foundation. Give these higher realms your attention and effort now.

What to Do: Connect to these symbols in various ways that call to you. Mindfully sketch them, print out their patterns and color them, or wear them as jewelry or patterns in your clothing.

Crystal Grids

A crystal grid is a great tool for connecting with your intuition, spiritual source energy, and the essence of the signs you've been receiving lately. First gather crystals, gemstones, or other objects such as leaves or shells you've been attracted to. Set an intention for your grid, either to connect better with the signs you've been getting, or to match the higher vibrations of the spirit surrounding you. Then, select a pattern grounded in sacred geometry. Now, arrange your materials in this pattern. You can meditate by your grid, activate it with chimes or a singing bowl, or leave it out in nature overnight to set your intention free.

Scorpion

A spiritual sign of letting go.

You may think that a creature with a venomous stinger would be feared throughout history, but the scorpion is actually widely revered! Its unique ability to protect itself as well as adapt to many harsh environments carries cross-cultural symbolism of determination, protection, and rebirth. When you see this symbol, you are being guided to let go of a negative and toxic element in your own life. A soul who has crossed over is empowering you to walk away from any people, places, and situations that no longer serve you. The transformation and rebirth of your own soul requires you to distance yourself from unhealthy circumstances—especially if you are experiencing loss and/or grief. You have the support of the other side as you let it all go.

What to Do: Be mindful today of anything that feels negative, toxic, or uncomfortable. Low vibrational frequencies, such as fair-weather friends, abusive situations, or places that make you feel unsettled, aren't necessary in your life anymore.

Shadow

A fleeting sign of a spirit.

A shadow that acts in a way that could be perceived as intelligent, seeks out your attention, and appears in places with no light at all may call for additional investigation. When a spirit comes to you as a shadow, it's actually a fleeting visitation! Usually these aren't souls you've known in life; rather, they are attached to the space you are occupying. They are often lingering bits of energy from those on the other side, which cling to objects or certain rooms in homes. A departed soul who enjoyed reading by their lamp each night may find themselves attached to the object long after they've left this world, or a soul who spent a lot of time roaming a certain hallway may have a lingering bit of energy still appear there. Learning about the history of the space, as well as any objects that a shadow visitor seems attached to, can help you understand this departed spirit and what they want. What may seem menacing or frightening at first is typically just a soulful presence looking for a path back to the other side. Luckily, you can help!

What to Do: Light a candle, burn incense, or practice any other spiritual ritual that feels comfortable for you. Open any windows in the space you have seen the shadow, then tell the presence out loud to "follow the light" to the other side. Finish this practice with a little light cleaning and/or prayer if it feels right. Going forward, you will most likely notice a decrease in the shadows you see in this space.

Shark

A symbol of support as you face your fears.

The shark is an apex predator in the ocean, compelling both fear and admiration from people throughout cultures and time. It is linked to numerous meanings, the most common being fearlessness, power, and protection. The shark has not evolved much throughout its eons of existence; it is a steady and adaptable force. Seeing this symbol is encouragement for you to embody the same strong vibration as the shark. You are being guided to face your fears with the intelligence and power you already possess. The other side is offering you protection as you do so.

What to Do: The situation that is causing you the most stress now is the one you'll need to reflect on. Think about how you are being controlled by your fears. What scares you most is what you are being asked to find a new perspective on. Reflect on how you can face your fear today in some small way.

Shell

A message of journey and transcendence.

Revered throughout time and history, the shell holds numerous meanings for many. The vessel that remains after life has passed through it is a reminder of your own temporary connection to the physical body. The shell can also represent change and protection, as it provides a space for a lot of different life-forms to find and use. Overall, the shell symbolizes the journey of one's life, the transcendence of a soul, and eternity. Seeing shells is a spiritual reminder to let go of material concerns and focus on your soulful journey instead. This sign often points to the eternal life you live through various forms.

What to Do: Incorporate shells and shell designs (art prints, drawer knobs, etc.) into a sacred space in your home. When you need a reminder of what is important, let the shell symbol guide you to your spiritual center.

Smoke

A sign of an established connection with the divine.

Seeing smoke rise from seemingly nowhere or smelling smoke when no fire or cigarette is in sight can be a sign from the other side. Smoke has many spiritual meanings. It represents purification, spiritual awakenings, and conversations with higher realms. When you are seeing smoke, it may be a spiritual presence attempting to connect with you. Smoke taking shape, following you, or floating midair is a way that souls manifest a form for your physical eyes to see. Smelling smoke can be a personal nudge from someone you know who has passed or a signal from a soul you haven't met but are being contacted by. Spirits will use your clairalience, or clear smelling, to boost your already existing sense of smell to communicate. You may sometimes smell the familiar scent of a cigar or pipe and associate that with a specific loved one. Smoke in dreams can often mean you are being awakened to more spiritual communication. In all cases, know that there is a strong and active connection with other side energy.

What to Do: Notice how the visions or odors of smoke arrive and disappear. A spiritual phenomenon doesn't linger; rather, it dissipates as quickly as it enters a room. When you sense this sign, consider your feelings, as these signals are loaded with emotional information.

Snake

A sign to encourage focus and hidden wisdom.

The fear and wonder that have always accompanied the snake are more than just impulsive reactions to this animal. Across many cultures, the snake has held a powerful symbolic meaning of transformation, protection, and spiritual introspection. Its recurring presence shows a need to concentrate and uncover the hidden wisdom buried deep within. The snake represents life cycles of both positive and negative experiences, all which bring you closer to your true self. When you see this symbol, the other side is encouraging you to focus on your own hidden wisdom. You are being called to uncover important truths about yourself and your perception of reality. There is a spiritual rebirth awaiting you when you find the answers you seek within.

What to Do: Nurture your inner wisdom today. Talk with a therapist or close friend, spend some time reflecting through journaling, or join a like-minded community that shares in your passions.

Song

A musical way for a departed loved one to reach your heart.

Hearing the favorite song of someone departed can immediately bring their essence to the present moment. Noticing this song playing in the background as you shop at the grocery store, pop up at the top of a playlist, or turn up in a montage sequence of the TV show you're watching isn't always a coincidence. Those who have crossed over will send you songs to bring your thoughts straight back to them. Lyrics also have special meaning to souls on the other side. Seeing lyrics of songs you associate with them in print and hearing the lyrics repeated by others, or even just playing over and over in your mind for no explicable reason, are signs that someone is trying to send you a heartfelt message of eternal connection.

What to Do: Set aside a time to play songs that remind you of your departed loved one. As you listen to the music, sit in your memories and know that the emotions you presently feel are shared by the one you miss so dearly.

Communicating Back: Make a Playlist

Making a list of songs that remind you of the departed can help you communicate with them. Add their favorite songs, or songs that had significance to both of you, as a way to bring their soul closer. Playing this song list will be emotional, not only for you but for those on the other side as well. Music is a conduit for emotion to move fluidly and unrestrained. This is the exact energy you need for connecting with souls who have crossed over. It can be difficult to sit in this type of intense memory, but it also comes with the reward of strong soulful contact. You can add songs that seem to be sent to you from the other side and also share this playlist with those you know will appreciate it.

Sparkles (In Your Line of Vision)

A glimpse of spiritual guidance.

Seeing sparkles, flashes of light, or other visual anomalies with no medical reason is usually a sign of ancestral or spiritual presence. Your third eye, or the space between your eyebrows, is in charge of your spiritual vision (seeing things beyond the physical realm). Those on the other side can activate your clairvoyance, or "clear seeing," through your third eye in order to heighten your awareness of them. Sparkles, flashes, or spots can alert you to a spiritual presence that has come to guide you.

What to Do: Notice when and where you are seeing these visual anomalies. Tap your third eye, meditate, and breathe mindfully while you visualize a healing light in the center of your forehead. In doing this, you are opening a portal to the spiritual vibrations that have come to lift you higher.

Communicating Back: Wear Meaningful Jewelry

Enhance that portal to the other side by wearing jewelry that once belonged to someone who has passed over. Metal in particular is a strong spiritual conduit, as it allows the energy of the departed to both give and receive emotion. Also notice when you choose a piece of the departed's jewelry to wear for bravery, protection, or simply because you miss them: This is a sign of your bond.

Sparrow

An inspirational message of loving protection.

The hardy sparrow that flutters in gardens and across fields is a busy little bird. Its courageous and hardworking nature has garnered much admiration throughout time and across different cultures. The sparrow is often associated with a divine provision, courage, contentment, and community. When you see a sparrow, know that a soul on the other side is comforting you and letting you know how protected you are, both by them and those around you. Despite the harshness of this world, you don't go unseen. Your humility and determination are inspirations to everyone who comes into contact with you! It's okay for you to receive the love you so freely give to others.

What to Do: Sit and reflect on where you have felt taken care of or protected lately. Think about how your connections with the community are helpful to your overall goals, as well as your emotional and physical well-being. There are people on this earth as well as in the unseen realms who take care of you.

Spider

A powerful signal to begin weaving your own destiny.

This intelligent creature builds marvelous webs of its own design. Innovative and motivated, the spider makes any space conducive to their survival. The spider has long been associated with curiosity, ingenuity, and personal growth. It shows that with patience and self-reliance, you can manifest your own reality. When you see this symbol, you are receiving a powerful sign to begin weaving your own destiny. Understanding what you want and creating it for yourself is not just possible, but something the other side urges you to do now. You are more than capable of doing it on your own; you don't need to wait for anyone else to help you.

What to Do: Think about something you have been recently wanting, such as a career that resonates with your soul, or a new home in which to thrive and grow. Begin manifesting this goal today by writing it down and placing the piece of paper somewhere you can see it often. Alternatively, you can make a note on your smartphone. When you allow this dream to exist in your reality, you can be more inspired and mindful of taking small steps toward it every day.

Squirrel

A cheerful symbol of spontaneity and adaptability.

The busy squirrel scurries up and down trees, gathering resources from all over—even the most unusual places. Yet it still makes sure to leave some time for playful adventures, such as chasing other squirrels and exploring new areas. When you see this symbol, you are being sent a message to make sure you leave some room for fun in your own life. There are many things you must do, but there are also ways you can include joy and laughter in your busy schedule. A soul on the other side sees how much you are doing, and they want you to get a little spontaneous and adaptable so that you can enjoy yourself too.

What to Do: Think about how you can add a little fun to your schedule today. Grab some ice cream on the way home from work, make a lunch date with a friend, or simply don a brightly colored sweater. You can be creative about how you spice up your daily life!

Stick Insect

A calming spiritual message about divine timing.

The stick insect remains motionless for long periods of time, effectively blending into its environment. For this reason, this insect is often a symbol of patience, adaptability, and stillness of mind. It is also associated with the ability to tap into inner intuition and skills of perception. When you see this symbol, you are being sent an otherworldly message that all things take time. It is sending you a calming energy, one that is meant to quell any anxious need you may have to rush through the natural process of what is to come. When you sit in stillness, you understand that all things come to you when they are meant to.

What to Do: Sit in stillness for a few moments. Allow yourself to breathe in and out slowly, connecting with your body, mind, and spirit. Notice when peace comes to you as you take this pause.

Swan

An acknowledgment of lasting love and spiritual awakening.

Gliding effortlessly across the water, the swan universally captures attention. The grace and allure of this bird have long been associated with love, beauty, and elegance. Because the swan mates for life, it represents loyalty and lasting commitment. Additionally, its ability to transform from such a little gray baby into its majestic adult form symbolizes metamorphosis and divine transcendence. When repeatedly confronted with this symbol, know that a spiritual source is giving you the message that the bond you share with them is eternal, and they are with you during your own soul's growth as they transition from this life to the next.

What to Do: Connect today with a friend or relative who understands the close bond you had shared with the departed. Feel their presence as you discuss the ways in which their influence shaped your lives.

Temperature/
Temperature Change

An atmospheric sign of spiritual presence.

Feeling a sudden dip or rise in temperature in one area of the room you are in, without any sort of rational explanation, is a common way for a spirit to make their presence known. The energy those on the other side manipulate in order for their soul to travel across realms can change the whole atmosphere of a room! You may find that as you walk through one area of a room, it is either freezing or very toasty—as if you were passing through an invisible wall that keeps one temperature in and another out. When you experience this temperature fluctuation, know that a soulful presence is with you in a powerful way.

What to Do: Check your clairsentience, or clear feeling, for any new emotions, bursts of energy, or sudden feelings of anxiety. As you enter and exit the space where the temperature changes, notice how you feel and who you sense is with you presently.

Feeling Flushed

When a spiritual presence is close by, it's not uncommon to receive a sudden rush of heat, discomfort, or sometimes even nausea. Their vibrational frequency is much different from your own; therefore, when they rush in to give a message, show their presence, or grab your attention, you may have an actual physical reaction. This can occur when you feel the need to take on a cause someone else left behind, when receiving your own signs from the spirit, or with complete strangers. For example, noticing that you feel this way when around a coworker who just lost her mother may not just be a sudden hot flash. You could be directed by the departed to deliver a message of her presence. Consider how you emotionally feel in these circumstances. You may find yourself wanting to ask the coworker about her family or give her a huge hug (if it's appropriate to your relationship). The combination of this flushed physical feeling plus the nagging need to show concern and support is a spirit using you to do their unfinished work.

Text

A communicative sign from the other side.

Receiving texts is an everyday occurrence; receiving texts from someone who has died, however, can make you pause. In the modern world of technological glitches, you may be tempted to pass this off as a simple phone network error—but it could be something a lot more meaningful! A text from a noteworthy phone number can be a significant message of communication from someone on the other side. You may notice that the phone number associated with the text is the departed's own number, or you may receive a text from an unknown contact that seems directed to you from someone who has crossed over. In any case, the communication is the sign itself. Phone communication, including texting, is symbolic of communication across realms. This person is physically not here, but can still make contact in their own spiritual ways. While this sign is commonly sent by loved ones, those who you may not know yet share another bond with may send you texts as well.

What to Do: Screenshot the text as a keepsake. Feel comfort in this soulful gesture of communication from the other side.

Tiger

A spiritual reminder to be in touch with your inner power.

Much like the animal itself, the tiger symbol is fierce. In many cultures, it represents power, strength, and strategy. The tiger is feared for the same reasons it is revered: It has abilities that many creatures of this world do not. You are seeing this symbol because someone on the other side is reminding you to get in touch with your own inner power. Untamed power is rash, unpredictable, and dangerous. Forgetting who you are and what you are capable of puts you at risk of falling behind in the goals and desires you deeply care about. It's time for you to remember exactly how powerful you are so you can begin to use that power accordingly.

What to Do: Get empowered today with mindful reflection and decisive action. Take some time to journal your feelings, sense where you are losing control in life, and make a plan for how to get that control back. You are mighty and fierce, and a spiritual source wants you to remember this.

Touch

A physical sign of a soulful presence.

The sensation of a hand running through your hair or a gentle caress on your shoulder when you're completely alone is a comfort those on the other side can bring you. While it's natural to be alarmed at first, you can calm your body's stress response by considering who may be present when this happens. Those on the other side can use their own energy as well as your clairsentience, or clear feeling senses, to create this new way of physical touch after they have crossed over. This is a favorite way to communicate for departed children, loved ones you knew well, or very strong spiritual energies you cohabitate with that seek your attention. It can be most noticeable in twilight states, or the space between being awake and asleep, where your body is more relaxed and spiritually attuned. These gentle touches may also be accompanied with feelings of peace, calm, and even at times whole body tingles.

What to Do: Look to your intuition for guidance in who is sending you these physical messages. Chances are you know exactly who is contacting you.

Communicating Back: Create a Gift in Their Name

Honoring someone who crossed over by assisting others who share the same passions they once did is a strong way to communicate with the other side. Naming a library after the librarian who devoted their life to their work, offering a college scholarship in a deceased community member's name, and creating a grant for a cause in honor of a passionate activist are just a few ways you can strengthen the bond between realms. Those who cross over are still concerned with the work they left behind on this physical plane. Allowing them a touchstone through this sort of proactive assistance in their memory helps them continue their work from the other side. Having their remembrance associated with inventions, devotions, and causes close to their hearts while they were living is a beautiful way to say, "Thank you."

Toy

A childlike symbol of innocence and joy.

A toy that lights up your inner child with wonder can also be used as a delightful sign from those who have crossed over! Encountering a toy that evokes nostalgia and a shared memory between you and the departed is one way for them to connect. Repeatedly seeing a similar type of toy over a period of time can be a communication of joy, creativity, and playfulness. You may even hear electronic toys turn on and off seemingly by themselves, or see them move when not being played with. Those on the other side are drawn to objects of such a high and happy vibration and will manipulate them to gain your attention. Toys are symbols of happiness, innocence, and the authenticity of who you are. Seeing this sign is a loving reminder of all your potential, as well as encouragement to live joyfully.

What to Do: Collect the toy that feels spiritually significant to you. Place it somewhere as a reminder to cherish the meaning it brings to you.

Tulip

A loved one's floral request that you remember them.

When someone crosses over, you grieve not just the loss of their presence, but also their unique self and personality. The tulip symbolizes hope, remembrance, and rebirth. Seeing it often in your life is a message from the departed that they are still fundamentally themselves, even though they now dwell on the other side. The beautiful things you remember about their personalities haven't changed.

What to Do: When you see this sign, sit in remembrance of how special the departed truly was. Think about their humor, what they loved to do, and the interesting stories they told. Bring them up in conversation when you feel comfortable doing so. They left a mark on this world, and when you speak of it, they are listening.

Flower Colors

The color of flowers can give additional meanings to signs. Different flowers carry their own colorful symbolism. Yellow roses depict friendship, while yellow tulips depict hope. The significance of the color will also differ based on the cultural context. In many Western cultures white flowers represent purity, while in many Eastern cultures they signify mourning. Mixing flower colors can also add an additional layer to the spiritual messages received. Orange and yellow flowers paired together can represent enthusiasm, while red and white signify unity.

Turkey

Spiritual advice to practice gratitude.

The turkey has an abundant spiritual presence in many cultures. This bird symbolizes generosity, growth, and rebirth. Gratitude is something you can forget to prioritize when you are deep within your grief. It can even feel like a betrayal of the departed's memory to think of anything positive in your life when you miss them so much. However, gratitude is a pathway through which those on the other side can connect with you. When you see the turkey symbol repeatedly, know that a soulful energy is asking you to practice gratitude in order to reach higher vibrations of communication within the spiritual world.

What to Do: Think of a few things you can be grateful for today. The friend who is always there for you, a cozy spot in your home, and even the first sip of coffee in the morning are wonderful reasons to feel thankful! Next, take a moment to reflect on what you have that could be shared with others. It could be as simple as a kind word or a dinner invite for a few friends. Extend this generosity now.

Turtle

A symbol encouraging you to ground yourself.

The gentle and slow-moving turtle plods along at its own pace, knowing that wherever it goes, home is right there on its back. The turtle has been a widespread symbol across many cultures and has powerful meanings. It is often associated with Mother Nature, wisdom, and tranquility. It is a reminder to stay steadfast on your life path, and slow down to make sure nothing goes unnoticed. When you see this symbol, you are receiving a sign from the other side encouraging you to ground yourself and practice feeling present in your own skin. Slowing down and centering within will allow you to evaluate all the choices you need to make in good time.

What to Do: Ground yourself in nature today by walking outside barefoot, sitting under a tree, or simply listening to the sounds nature has to offer. When you pay attention to nature, you find the voice within you speaks louder.

Violet

A floral nod to the transience of life.

This life can seem cold, hard, and entirely too long after loss. But those on the other side want you to know that it's important to see the beauty around you, even when you are feeling trapped in the darkness. The violet is a symbol of the transience of life, as well as remembrance, loyalty, and serenity. It is tied to higher consciousness—the part of you that relies on emotion and intuition. When you see this flower, know that the departed is asking you to find some value to this life while you are still living it. Just like the violet itself, life is beautiful and delicate. Cherish it.

What to Do: Take a moment and focus on one thing that is beautiful in life today. It could be the way the light streams through your window in the morning, or the beautiful tree you pass by every day but haven't taken the time to appreciate before. No matter how seemingly small this object or moment you're focusing on is, know that when you give it your attention, a spiritual source is right there with you.

Communicating Back: Gift Flowers

Giving flowers is always a thoughtful sentiment, and you can give flowers to communicate with those on the other side! There are a few ways you can use flowers to kick off a spiritual correspondence. Sending flowers with symbolic meaning to a person who recently experienced a loss can become a conduit for other-side messages. Feeling the need to send a certain flower to a bereaved friend could facilitate a significant message from their loved one. This can also be a way to communicate with your own soulful connections. Gifting your departed's favorite flower to honor them—either as a hostess gift, a kind gesture, or a way to brighten up a coworker's day—is a little "wink" to their spiritual presence and can be a fun exchange between you and the other side.

Vision (Seeing)

A visual symbol of a soul's presence.

A figure suddenly standing in a doorway, walking down a hall, or appearing outside a window would stop anyone in their tracks—especially if this vision evaporates not long after you see it. But this startling occurrence could be an important sign from beyond. It takes a lot of energy for souls to appear to you. Additionally, your third eye (or the spiritual eye between your eyebrows) must be activated enough for you to see this phenomenon. Whether or not you know the person who is showing themselves, they are purposefully doing so to get your attention. You may see distinct facial features or fuzzy outlines. This occurrence will most certainly prompt strong emotional and physical reactions: These are important to note, as they will help you decipher the messages of the departed.

What to Do: Explore the significance of this vision by investigating the bond between you and the one who has appeared.

Communicating Back: Pass On Their Name

Those on the other side are particularly connected to namesakes and feel called to protect those named after them, even if they have never met in the physical world. Naming a baby after a loved one who has left this world is a beautiful way to honor them. Naming a property such as a home, business, or piece of land after the departed brings their energy forward with a similar watchfulness.

Wasp

A protective sign urging you to be proactive.

Hearing the buzzing of a wasp can cause an instinctive reaction to run away. But while the wasp inspires alarm in many, it actually symbolizes protection, diligence, and the need to be wary of present situations. It points to potentially dangerous circumstances and encourages mindful behavior. When noticing this sign in your life, a spiritual presence is urging you to reconsider conditions around you and be proactive in your own self-preservation. Carry the productive and resilient energy of the wasp into your daily life.

What to Do: Consider any current conflicts, relationships, or ongoing situations. Perhaps it's time to stop procrastinating on a legal issue, or make the necessary changes to a negative relationship dynamic that has been escalating. Reflect on where you could be more proactive in researching all angles of this issue and protecting yourself.

Water (As a Paranormal Conduit)

A conduit for soulful signals.

Water is of the utmost importance to the existence of life in this realm, and because of this, it holds layers of significance for both the living and departed. In a symbolic sense, it represents cleansing, rebirth, and divine grace. For those on the other side, physical bodies of water also provide favorable conditions for them to make their presence known. Finding yourself more aware of signs, messages, and even visuals from souls can be easier while near a lake or an ocean. Even while in the bath or shower, you may find elevated clarity and connection to the spirit. Water is often a place where both the departed and living can unite in order to send and receive insight and feel close.

What to Do: Meditate near a body of water with the intention of reaching out to departed souls. Be open to what comes to your mind at this time, as it may be spiritual messages from the other side.

Water (In Dreams)

A sign of your spiritual relationships.

Dreaming about water can be a soulful signal to the relationship you have with your own spirituality. Pay attention to the depth, clarity, as well as speed of the water in your dream to indicate what messages are being conveyed. For example, feeling swept up in a fast river may signify a need to contemplate your own spiritual beliefs, while being dipped in stagnant, muddy water may alert you to immediate changes needed in your active connection to the spirit. Deep, bottomless water may suggest there is a lot to uncover in your discovery of self, whereas shallow pools may be symbolic of the need to dig a bit deeper into your subconscious thoughts.

What to Do: Journal about your dreams that involve water. Consider the layered meanings of these dreams and how they may relate to your present circumstances. Contemplate what advice the spirit may be giving you through these dreams.

Communicating Back: Invite Spiritual Dreams

Your dreams are the perfect landing place for spiritual communication. Place significant crystals such as labradorite under your pillow to welcome soulful energy, wear an item of the departed's clothing or keep a personal effect of theirs near your bed, directly ask spiritual energy to come through, or meditate on the spiritual connection before sleep.

Water (In House/Leak/Dripping)

An inconvenient sign of a soulful conduit.

Leaking faucets, burst pipes, and other plumbing problems aren't always just a fact of life. At times, they are indications that a spiritual presence is attempting to make itself known to you. Water is an especially strong conduit for spiritual communication, and when there is a soulful presence in a home with you, their (often well-intended) need to stay connected to the property or to you may result in some very unwanted plumbing bills. The influx of problems as well as a professional opinion that this is a bit excessive will allow you to determine if the solution may be more paranormal than practical.

What to Do: If you do decide that these issues are aggravated by an otherworldly guest, search for other ways they can communicate. Decorate with some chimes or candles delegated just for their use.

Water Fountains

You can also invite more spiritual conversations (and deter those on the other side from using plumbing issues to do so) with a fountain. Whether it is a small indoor fountain or a more elaborate outdoor version, creating this space draws the attention of the departed. Making a daily habit of meditating near this new focal point will give those on the other side room to work. You may see an uptick of spiritual activity around the home.

Weather Fluctuation

Affirmation of a soul's presence near you.

Connecting with nature is one way to tap into your already existing ability to get in touch with those on the other side. Sudden sun showers, a random snow flurry, and beaming sun rays encircling you in their shimmering embrace are sometimes signs from a spiritual energy, cluing you in to their presence. Specifically, sun showers are often a reassurance that nothing is permanent, snow flurries signal a need to let go of the past, and sun rays, or "God lights," are seen as a direct interaction with the divine. When experiencing these sudden weather fluctuations, you may feel a sense of your own soul lifting and rising to meet the heavenly vibrations, a wave of pure elation washing over you. You can feel loved, whole, and filled with gratitude. A strong spiritual energy is sending you a special message saying, "I am here with you."

What to Do: Pay special attention to what you were doing, thinking, and reminiscing about just as the weather fluctuation occurred. Take hold of the emotions you were just given in this moment of connection with nature and the spiritual realm, and try to recreate these feelings throughout the rest of the day.

Whale

A symbol guiding you toward your spiritual awakening.

Majestic and awe inspiring, the whale has been revered by many cultures and carries a lot of powerful symbolic meanings. The whale sign is often seen as reflecting your own connection to the divine. It also represents wisdom, protection, and an inner voice as its songs are thought to be connected to the unseen realms. When you are consistently drawn to this symbol, a soulful energy on the other side is guiding you toward your spiritual awakening. There is a relationship you need to strengthen with the unseen realms, and now is the time to do it. When you listen to the voice within you, you can pick up more of the signs and messages of the ones who've crossed over.

What to Do: Ask yourself where you may feel curious to dive deeper into your connection with your own intuition. You may feel compelled to study a spiritual practice such as tarot or astrology, journal your dreams, or simply be more mindful of the intuitive impulses that you've previously shrugged off. Pay closer attention to all your thoughts and feelings moving forward: They carry important spiritual messages from those on the other side.

Whispering

An audible sign of a soul's presence.

Hearing hushed whispers when you are sure you are completely alone may be a sign that you have more company than you think. Muffled conversations, your whispered name, and soft voices in the background are all signs of souls wanting to make themselves known. Those who have crossed over will work with your clairaudience, or clear hearing, to allow you to "hear" the world beyond. When hearing the audible signs of whispers directed toward you, take them as a positive indication that a soul or two is very interested in speaking to you.

What to Do: When noticing an uptick in these phantom whispers, talk directly to whoever you feel is speaking. Ask them questions out loud and see what answers you get back, either audibly or intuitively.

Communicating Back: Share Their History

When you share history, those on the other side who feel connected to what you are saying come through strongly. Giving a tour of a historical site, visiting schools to teach about a past local event, and answering visitors' questions at a museum are never things you do alone: Those who have crossed over enjoy having their stories told! The things they valued, fought for, and loved are still important to them in their new forms.

Willow (Leaf/Tree)

A harmonious sign from a spirit.

Delicate branches of draped leaves bend and sway in the wind. The willow tree has various cultural interpretations as it grows in many different landscapes and climates. Often, it holds symbolism for emotional healing, resilience, and the harmony of the natural world. It has been long sought after as a tree of comfort in trying times—a reminder that adaptability is the key component to living harmoniously. When you see this tree or leaf symbolism, know that spiritual energy is urging you to restore lost hope by embracing the present moment as is. The cycles of life in all their ebbs and flows are part of a larger picture, and you are one with all of it.

What to Do: Consider where you can restore your hope in life and feel in harmony once again. Meditate on what you are grateful for and/or spend time in nature and with those who lift your spirits.

Communicating Back: Preserve Leaves

Collecting fallen leaves that have spiritual meaning to you is one way to celebrate your bonds on the other side. When noticing leaves you feel are symbolic and special, you can preserve them not only as a beautiful form of artistic expression, but also to safeguard the spiritual message they intend. Taking the time to place meaningful leaves into a leaf press, or using another medium for preservation such as wax, facilitates a new sort of conversation with the ones who sent these special signs. You are acknowledging the message they bring and honoring it with the effort spent keeping it near you. Place the leaves around your home as decor or in a space of distinction such as on a mantle. Seeing them daily and taking a moment to consider the ways in which you received them is a powerful exchange between you and those who have left this realm.

Wishing Stone

A reminder that spiritual connection is a simple wish away.

Smooth coastal stones adorned with a faint line of quartz are often called wishing stones. Cross-culturally, the wishing stone carries many spiritual meanings and is universally treasured for holding symbolic significance. The line of quartz symbolizes the bridge of connection to the other side, and can even be a geological conduit for soulful communication. Running your finger down the line of quartz while stating an intention is thought to reverberate that thought into the ethereal realms, so it gets more attention and can be better honored. If you are noticing wishing stones everywhere or feel that a certain one connects you to a soul on the other side, it's quite possible it was put in your path for that very reason.

What to Do: Hold the stone carefully in your hand and run your fingers along the quartz line in its center. Call on the other side and state your intention. You could ask to connect with a loved one or receive advice from ancestors, or request assistance from the other side. Sit with your emotions for a moment and open yourself to whatever comes next.

Wolf

A symbol of fierce loyalty.

The wolf has long embodied loyalty and protection, and it is a symbol that has profound meanings in many cultures. Working closely with members of a pack, the wolf counts on its community for survival. It also represents leadership, instinct, and the need to make one's voice heard. When you see this symbol, a spiritual energy is letting you know that their loyalty lies with you always. Know that as you make your own way, you have the support of those on the other side. You are being encouraged to speak your truth and to stand in confidence with your beliefs. There are people who may judge you, but the spirit is with you.

What to Do: Reflect carefully on where you are feeling alone and isolated. The places and situations that aren't welcoming to you may need to be reevaluated.

Woodpecker

A spiritual reassurance that nothing is random; signs are everywhere.

Making its home in wooded habitats, the woodpecker is a long-standing symbol of perseverance, inner strength, and determination. It carefully observes its environment and makes its way with adaptability and inner wisdom. When you see this symbol, a soulful energy is asking you to pay close attention to your surroundings. The people you meet, opportunities you encounter, and intuitions you feel while navigating them are all tools for your survival and success. Feathers in your path, a seemingly random message from a stranger, and a flower that captures your attention are all ways you could be signaled by divine energy. Those on the other side are speaking to you through many channels, and finding patterns in them will be revealing for you.

What to Do: Think about the recent occurrences in your life and reflect on what bigger picture you may be able to see. Have any small symbolic coincidences collided with larger life milestones? Make the conscious decision to pay attention to your surroundings throughout your day, and congratulate yourself whenever you notice a sign!

Bird Feeder

A bird feeder is an excellent way to encourage signs sent by feathery messengers! Set up your bird feeder in a peaceful, calming space where you can easily see it. Incorporate some bird watching into your routine each day so you can notice the signs and pick up on happy feelings from the spirits communicating with you. You may want to put a feeder outside your office window to see as you work, in front of your kitchen window where you do dishes, or in a spot where it's easy to sit in peace and quiet with your morning coffee. Notice the feelings you have when you see different birds visit, and any emotions or visions that come to you as you watch. You can also keep a log of birds you see to better notice patterns and other meaningful details, such as a specific bird visiting you on a significant date.

Wreath

A visual representation of deep symbolic significance.

The wreath has held deep significance for religious ceremonies and cultural celebrations across time. Universally speaking, the wreath symbolizes the circle of life, hope, and prosperity. However, it often has varied symbolism depending upon which materials are used to create it, as well as the season or celebration it is used for. Wreaths of pine or evergreen are often a call back to the everlasting life of the soul, whereas wheat indicates prosperity. A wreath during harvest times can mean gratitude and abundance, while winter wreaths convey strength and hope. When you are finding yourself noticing an abundance of wreaths, know that a spiritual energy is giving you a visual representation of deep significance. Taking further consideration of a wreath's color and materials and its celebratory or cultural context will provide you with a more personalized message.

What to Do: Note the plants, flowers, fruits, and colors of the wreaths you've been encountering and what these different materials could mean. Notice any patterns over time.

Zinnia

**A floral message from a departed loved one
of transcendence and tribute.**

When enduring the devastating grief after loss, it can be hard to see how you could find a pathway to joy ever again. But grief, just like joy, isn't permanent. The zinnia is associated with remembrance, tribute, and the transition of sadness into happiness. In the layered depth of your emotions, you will find that the level of pain directly relates to the abundance of love you shared with the departed. The memory of those who've passed may be painful to recall, but it is essential for maintaining the connection between you and the departed; it also aids in keeping your heart open to more happiness in the future. The zinnia is a sign from a departed loved one saying, "Remember me." Remembering them in the smallest ways is how you honor their spirit and allow a little light to shine through the darkness of pain.

What to Do: Keep your loved one in mind today when seeing this flower. Talk to them in your head, sharing stories from your day and letting them know you're thinking about the good times you shared together.

PART 3

Signs Log

Patterns play an important role in interpreting spiritual signs. The signs you are receiving become more and more significant based on their frequency, setting, and emotional impact. Additionally, documenting the signs and their messages in detail gives that much more space and attention to the voice of the departed person communicating with you. In this part, you will find a template to help you record and reflect on the special messages you receive.

Using the provided Signs Log pages, you will be able to keep track of each specific sign you have observed, along with the date, a summary of its meaning, and your own intuitive perception of what it means. Combining your observations with your emotions will help preserve the experience of seeing a sign and keep it vivid in your memory. This is particularly important because those who have crossed over thrive in being remembered and can build on past messages to send new ones. This log will not only be your record of the past, but also work as a foundation for more spiritual connections in the future! Once you have filled up the logs in this part, you can continue tracking signs by repeating the template in a separate notebook or on a notes app on your smartphone. Let's get started.

Today's Encounter

Sign:

Where You Saw It:

When You Saw It
(Date/Time):

Sign Meaning:

Reflection:

Today's Encounter

Sign:

Where You Saw It:

When You Saw It (Date/Time):

Sign Meaning:

Reflection:

Today's Encounter

Sign:

Where You Saw It:

When You Saw It (Date/Time):

Sign Meaning:

Reflection:

Today's Encounter

Sign:

Where You Saw It:

When You Saw It (Date/Time):

Sign Meaning:

Reflection:

Today's Encounter

Sign:

Where You Saw It:

When You Saw It
(Date/Time):

Sign Meaning:

Reflection:

Today's Encounter

Sign:

Where You Saw It:

When You Saw It (Date/Time):

Sign Meaning:

Reflection:

Today's Encounter

Sign:

Where You Saw It:

When You Saw It (Date/Time):

Sign Meaning:

Reflection:

Today's Encounter

Sign:

Where You Saw It:

When You Saw It (Date/Time):

Sign Meaning:

Reflection:

Today's Encounter

Sign:

Where You Saw It:

When You Saw It (Date/Time):

Sign Meaning:

Reflection:

Today's Encounter

Sign:

Where You Saw It:

When You Saw It (Date/Time):

Sign Meaning:

Reflection:

Today's Encounter

Sign:

Where You Saw It:

When You Saw It (Date/Time):

Sign Meaning:

Reflection:

Today's Encounter

Sign:

Where You Saw It:

When You Saw It (Date/Time):

Sign Meaning:

Reflection:

Today's Encounter

Sign:

Where You Saw It:

When You Saw It
(Date/Time):

Sign Meaning:

Reflection:

Today's Encounter

Sign:

Where You Saw It:

When You Saw It (Date/Time):

Sign Meaning:

Reflection:

Today's Encounter

Sign:

Where You Saw It:

When You Saw It
(Date/Time):

Sign Meaning:

Reflection:

Today's Encounter

Sign:

Where You Saw It:

When You Saw It (Date/Time):

Sign Meaning:

Reflection:

Today's Encounter

Sign:

Where You Saw It:

When You Saw It
(Date/Time):

Sign Meaning:

Reflection:

Today's Encounter

Sign:

Where You Saw It:

When You Saw It
(Date/Time):

Sign Meaning:

Reflection:

Today's Encounter

Sign:

Where You Saw It:

When You Saw It (Date/Time):

Sign Meaning:

Reflection:

Index

About the Author

Mystic Michaela (Megan Firester) is a fourth-generation psychic medium. Her true passion is guiding people through Spirit to live their own authentic lives. Michaela currently resides in South Florida, where she has a thriving practice of personal clients. She is also the host of her own podcast, *Know Your Aura with Mystic Michaela*. She has been featured as a New Age expert in *Well+Good, Cosmopolitan, Shape, Women's Health, Elle,* and more.